CONTEMPORARY WRITERS

General Editors
MALCOLM BRADBURY
and
CHRISTOPHER BIGSBY

THOMAS PYNCHON

THOMAS
PYNCHON

TONY TANNER

METHUEN
LONDON AND NEW YORK

For Frank Kermode

First published in 1982 by
Methuen & Co. Ltd
11 New Fetter Lane, London EC4P 4EE
Published in the USA by
Methuen & Co.
in association with Methuen, Inc.
733 Third Avenue, New York, NY 10017
© 1982 Tony Tanner
Typeset by Rowland Phototypesetting Ltd
Printed in Great Britain by
Richard Clay (The Chaucer Press) Ltd
Bungay, Suffolk

British Library Cataloguing in Publication Data

Tanner, Tony
Thomas Pynchon. – (Contemporary writers)
1. Pynchon, Thomas – Criticism and interpretation
I. Title   II. Series
813'.54   PS3566.Y55Z/

ISBN 0-416-31670-0

Library of Congress Cataloging in Publication Data

Tanner, Tony
Thomas Pynchon.
(Contemporary writers)
Bibliography: P.
1. Pynchon, Thomas – Criticism and interpretation.
I. Title.   II. Series
PS3566.Y55Z9   813'.54   81-22534
ISBN 0-416-31670-0 (pbk.)   AACR2

CONTENTS

GENERAL EDITORS' PREFACE

Over the past twenty years or so, it has become clear that a decisive change has taken place in the spirit and character of contemporary writing. There now exists around us, in fiction, drama and poetry, a major achievement which belongs to our experience, our doubts and uncertainties, our ways of perceiving – an achievement stylistically radical and novel, and likely to be regarded as quite as exciting, important and innovative as that of any previous period. This is a consciousness and a confidence that has grown very slowly. In the 1950s it seemed that, somewhere amidst the dark realities of the Second World War, the great modernist impulse of the early years of this century had exhausted itself, and that the post-war arts would be arts of recessiveness, pale imitation, relative sterility. Some, indeed, doubted the ability of literature to survive the experiences of holocaust. A few major figures seemed to exist, but not a style or a direction. By the 1960s the confidence was greater, the sense of an avant-garde returned, the talents multiplied, and there was a growing hunger to define the appropriate styles, tendencies and forms of a new time. And by the 1970s it was not hard to see that we were now surrounded by a remarkable, plural, innovative generation, indeed several layers of generations, whose works represented a radical inquiry into contemporary forms and required us to read and understand – or, often, to read and *not* understand – in quite new ways. Today, as the 1980s start, that cumulative post-war achievement has acquired a degree of coherence that allows for critical response and understanding; hence the present series.

We thus start it in the conviction that the age of Beckett, Borges, Nabokov, Bellow, Pynchon, Robbe-Grillet, Golding, Murdoch, Fowles, Grass, Handke and Calvino, of Albee, Mamet, Shepard, Ionesco, Orton, Pinter and Stoppard, of Ginsberg, Lowell, Ashbery, Paz, Larkin and Hughes, and many another, is indeed an outstanding age of international creation, striking experiment, and some degree of aesthetic coherence. It is a time that has been described as 'post-modern', in the sense that it is an era consequent to modernism yet different from it, having its own distinctive preoccupations and stylistic choices. That term has its limitations, because it is apt to generate too precise definitions of the contemporary experiment, and has acquired rather too specific associations with contemporary American writing; but it does help concentrate our sense of living in a distinctive period. With the new writing has come a new criticism or rather a new critical theorem, its thrust being 'structuralist' or 'deconstructive' – a theorem that not only coexists with but has affected that writing (to the point where many of the best theorists write fictions, the best fictionalists write criticism). Again, its theory can be hermetic and enclosing, if not profoundly apocalyptic; but it points to the presence in our time of a new sense of the status of word and text, author and reader, which shapes and structures the making of modern form.

The aim of 'Contemporary Writers' is to consider some of the most important figures in this scene, looking from the standpoint of and at the achievement of the writers themselves. Its aims are eclectic, and it will follow no tight definition of the contemporary; it will function on the assumption that contemporary writing is by its nature multidirectional and elusive, since styles and directions keep constantly changing in writers who, unlike the writers of the past, are continuous, incomplete, not dead (though several of these studies will address the careers of those who, though dead, remain our contemporaries, as many of those who continue to write are manifestly not). A fair criticism of living writers must be assertive but also provisional, just as a fair sense of contemporary style must be open to that most crucial of contemporary awarenesses, that of the suddenness of change. We do not assume, then, that there is one right path to contemporary experiment, nor that a self-conscious reflexiveness, a deconstructive strategy, an art of

7

performance or a metafictional mode is the only one of current importance. As Iris Murdoch said, 'a strong agile realism which is of course not photographic naturalism' – associated perhaps especially with British writing, but also with Latin-American and American – is also a major component of modern style.

So in this series we wish to identify major writers, some of whom are avant-garde, others who are familiar, even popular, but all of whom are in some serious sense contemporary and in some contemporary sense serious. The aim is to offer brief, lucid studies of their work which draw on modern theoretical issues but respond, as much modern criticism does not, to their distinctiveness and individual interest. We have looked for contributors who are engaged with their subjects – some of them being significant practising authors themselves, writing out of creative experience, others of whom are critics whose interest is personal as well as theoretical. Each volume will provide a thorough account of the author's work so far, a solid bibliography, a personal judgement – and, we hope, an enlarged understanding of writers who are important, not only because of the individual force of their work, but because they are ours in ways no past writer could really be.

Norwich, England, 1981
MALCOLM BRADBURY
CHRISTOPHER BIGSBY

ACKNOWLEDGEMENTS

A short part of one section of this monograph appeared in *Salmagundi* (Fall, 1976). I am grateful to the editors for allowing me to reprint it.

I should like to express my gratitude to my research student, John Dugdale, with whom I have had many rewarding conversations concerning Thomas Pynchon.

The author and publisher would like to thank the following for permission to reproduce copyright material: Thomas Pynchon, J. B. Lippincott Company and Jonathan Cape Ltd for extracts from *The Crying of Lot 49* and *V.*; Thomas Pynchon, Viking Press and Jonathan Cape Ltd for extracts from *Gravity's Rainbow*.

A NOTE ON THE TEXTS

Page references in this book are to the following editions:

V.	Harmondsworth: Penguin, 1966
The Crying of Lot 49	London: Bantam Books, 1967
Gravity's Rainbow	New York: Viking Press, 1973

1

THOMAS PYNCHON AND THE DEATH OF THE AUTHOR

Some years ago there was much talk of 'the death of the author' – not his literal death but rather the necessary disconnection of the author and his life from whatever texts bear his name. Roland Barthes's essay on 'The Death of the Author' (1968) may be taken as representative. I quote from that influential work:

> Writing is that neutral, composite, oblique space where our subject slips away, the negative where all identity is lost, starting with the very identity of the body writing. . . . The image of literature to be found in ordinary culture is tyrannically centred on the author, his person, his life, his tastes, his passions. . . . The *explanation* of a work is always sought in the man or woman who produced it, as if it were always in the end, through the more or less transparent allegory of the fiction, the voice of a single person, the *author* 'confiding' in us. . . . Linguistically, the author is never more than the instance writing. . . . His only power is to mix writings, to counter the ones with the others, in such a way as never to rest on any of them . . . a text is made up of multiple writings, drawn from many cultures and entering into mutual relations of dialogue, parody, contestation, but there is one place where this multiplicity is focused and that place is the reader, not, as was hitherto said, the author. The reader is the space on which all the quotations that make up a writing are inscribed without any of them being lost; a text's unity lies not in its origin but in its destination . . . the birth of the reader must be at the cost of the death of the author.[1]

Not all of this will seem very new to many of us: at least since the advent of the 'New Criticism' the attention of the critic has been on the text rather than on the author, and the creative role of the reader has been increasingly stressed (for example, by such critics as Wolfgang Iser). Indeed, perhaps the first important writer to produce a theory of fiction already made that point. Thus Henry James writing about George Eliot in 1866:

> In every novel the work is divided between the writer and the reader: but the writer makes the reader very much as he makes his own characters. When he makes him ill, that is indifferent, he does no work; the writer does all. When he makes him well, that is, makes him interested, then the reader does quite half the labour.

The relevance of these considerations to Thomas Pynchon, who has managed to 'disappear' not only from his work but almost quite literally, will I hope become clear. No contemporary writer has achieved such fame and such anonymity at the same time, and arguably no other contemporary writer has done so much to create – or bring to birth – a new kind of reader who must do 'quite half the labour'. But before saying a little about Pynchon as 'author' – 'his person, his life', if not 'his tastes, his passions' – I want to draw attention to a persistent strain in the writing of American authors which reveals a suspicion of all kinds of 'biography' and a growing hostility to 'publicity' (and it should be remembered that America effectively invented mass publicity, starting in the early nineteenth century). As early as 1838 James Fenimore Cooper was inveighing against the power of the press in *The American Democrat*:

> If newspapers are useful in overthrowing tyrants, it is only to establish a tyranny of their own. . . . As the press of this country now exists, it would seem to be expressly devised by the great agent of mischief, to depress and destroy all that is good, and to elevate and advance all that is evil in the nation.[2]

Henry James wrote *The Reverberator* (1888) to attack the destructive influence of the press, to take on 'a type of newspaper man, a man whose ideal is the energetic reporter. I should like to *bafouer* the vulgarity and hideousness of this, the impudent invasion of privacy, the extinction of all conception of privacy, etc.' When Henry Adams sent his *Education* (1907) to James he wrote: 'This volume is a mere shield of protection in the grave. I advise you to take your own life in the same way, in order to prevent biographers from taking it in theirs.'

Well, such dedicated biographers as Ernest Samuels and Leon Edel have 'taken' those lives in their own way – and a very scholarly and interesting way it is too. But I am more concerned with an attitude, an attitude perhaps most succinctly summed up by Emily Dickinson when she wrote: 'Biography first convinces us of the fleeing of the Biographied.'[3] Now I suggest that all this is not to be attributed to patrician hauteur, aristocratic dislike of the popular press, a sense of reticence, a respect for privacy, a modesty, even a *pudeur* – though of course any and all of these may contribute to that antipathy to the notion of the exposure of the author's actual life. More generally I think there is a dislike for publicity in the way that it can take over a writer's life and manipulate and exploit it, turning it into a saleable image, so that the 'life' and the works may become confused, or the life becomes the dominant 'fiction' to which the writer may succumb (Hemingway is arguably an instance of this), to the detriment – or ignoring – of the imaginative 'life' contained in the work.

I am not suggesting that this attitude or suspicion is unique among American writers; of course it is not. But in no other country has a successful writer had to contend so much with the problems attendant upon 'publicity' – of being in one way or another 'consumed' by the public. (For the unsuccessful writer there may be only an annihilating absence of attention.) A writer like Norman Mailer has made a career out of accepting these conditions; it might be said that he lives *in* public, lives *off* publicity, asserting his hyper-visible ego, intruding it into all manner of public occasions from boxing matches to political conventions, competitively 'advertising' himself in a culture dominated by advertising at every level. Arguably – cause and effect are notoriously difficult to estimate in such cases – both his successes and his failures are the consequence of the risks of this enterprise. With Pynchon it has been all the other way. He became famous and invisible at almost the same moment (more invisible than the 'invisible poet', T. S. Eliot, well masked though he was). I would not presume to offer reasons (I *could* not) for this almost total abdication. To my knowledge it is unique among famous contemporary writers; even the eremetic Samuel Beckett is comparatively more known, more 'seen', even more photographed than Pynchon. (That last point may seem utterly trivial, but is there any other modern author of whom there is only one known photograph?) I think Pynchon's 'disappearance' does have a relevance to his work, in ways that I hope may emerge, albeit indirectly. But first I want to survey what little 'biographical' material seems to be available, while still bearing in mind 'the fleeing of the Biographied'.

I know of three attempts to set down some 'facts' about Thomas Pynchon, man and author (and if I put 'facts' in inverted commas it is because it seems that very little can be known for certain in this area). I shall draw on these for what seem to me potentially relevant considerations. In 'The Quest for Pynchon' Matthew Winston traces the family back to one Thomas Ruggles Pynchon of the eleventh century.[4] In 1630 a descendant named William Pynchon brought the family to the New World. In 1650 William published a tract entitled *The Meritorious Price of our Redemption*. In Winston's words, 'The book asserts that Christ saved mankind through his perfect obedience to God, not through Adam's curse, that "Christ did not suffer for us those unutterable torments of God's wrath, that commonly are called Hell-torments, to redeem our soules from them".' This work was not to the liking of the dominant New England Puritans, and it was condemned to be burned. William returned to England. (Arguably a version of this ancestor appears as William Slothrop in *Gravity's Rainbow*.)

The name Pyncheon occurs, of course, in Hawthorne's *The House of the Seven Gables*, and Hawthorne was surprised to receive letters of complaint from members of the Pynchon family. One of those who wrote to him was the Rev. Thomas Ruggles Pynchon (1823–1904), who taught chemistry, geology, zoology and theology at Trinity College, Hartford. The grand-nephew of that Pynchon became the father of Thomas Ruggles Pynchon, the novelist we are considering, who was born on 8 May 1937 in Glen Cove, Long Island, New York. He won a scholarship to Cornell University where he first studied engineering physics, but, after a spell in the navy, he returned to the College of Arts and Sciences and took his degree in English.

14

He received his BA in June 1960 'with distinction in all subjects'. While at Cornell, he was on the editorial staff of its undergraduate literary magazine, *The Cornell Writer*, in which he published his first piece of fiction; he also wrote some other short stories during this time (about all of which, more later). After graduating he lived in Greenwich Village, Manhattan, and went to work for the Boeing Company in Seattle, Washington (1960–2). He then lived in California and Mexico while finishing his novel, *V.*, which appeared in 1963 and was awarded the William Faulkner Foundation Award for the best first novel of the year. Since then: rumours; no interviews, no public appearances, no pictures.

His latest novel, *Gravity's Rainbow*, was published in 1973 and was nominated for three major literary prizes. It shared the National Book Award with a collection of stories by Isaac Bashevis Singer. Pynchon did not appear at the presentation: in his place a comedian appeared to accept the prize, and confuse the audience. It was elected by the judges for the Pulitzer Prize, a decision that was overruled by the Pulitzer advisory board (who found the book both 'unreadable' and 'obscene'). In 1975 the book was awarded the Howells Medal, which Pynchon declined, suggesting it be given to some other author. He wrote:

> The Howells Medal is a great honor, and, being gold, probably a good hedge against inflation too. But I don't want it. Please don't impose on me something I don't want. It makes the Academy look arbitrary and me look rude. . . . I know I should behave with more class, but there appears to be only one way to say no, and that's no.

And that's Pynchon.

A more colloquial and less informative piece appeared in *Playboy* (March 1971), in which Jules Siegel reminisced about Pynchon under the somewhat egregious title 'Who is Thomas Pynchon and why did he take off with my wife?'. Siegel was at Cornell with Pynchon in 1954 and offers such details as: 'Tom Pynchon was quiet and neat and did his homework faithfully. He went to Mass and confessed, though to what would be a mystery.' It is not surprising to read that Pynchon was 'a very private person'. Given the use made of teeth in *V.*, it is perhaps of mild interest to learn that Pynchon was 'ashamed' of his teeth and had 'extensive and painful dental restoration' done in Mexico City. Apparently in a letter he referred to his 'misshapen choppers' and said that they had 'determined his life in some unspecified way that seemed very important to him'.

More pertinent is the assertion that Pynchon's mother was a Catholic and was, if not anti-Semitic, not keen on having her children 'surrounded with Jews'. His father was, apparently, Protestant. At Cornell – so Siegel asserts – Pynchon had a Jewish girlfriend. The somewhat dubious relevance of all this is that a number of Pynchon's characters are of mixed religions: for example, Cleanth Siegel (note the name – Jules Siegel says that some people thought the character was based on him) in Pynchon's story 'Mortality and Mercy in Vienna' and Benny Profane in *V.* are both half-Jewish and half-Catholic; and the mysterious metamorphosing woman referred to as 'V.' is a Roman Catholic of a rather peculiar kind. (I might insert here a personal anecdote. While attending a conference on contemporary Jewish writers I was assured by an American female Jewish writer that Pynchon was Jewish. She had no evidence to substantiate this claim but clearly believed that it was – well – simply obvious. It seems quite clear that he is not – the moral being, perhaps, that given the catholicity and range of sympathy and interest manifest in Pynchon's work 'he' can seem to be, by selective inference, whatever or whomsoever you want to see him to be.)

One more reminiscence from Siegel. He apparently complained about the 'complexity' of *V.*: to which, in a letter, Pynchon retorted, 'Why should things be easy to understand?' We shall return to the matter of 'complexity' and 'difficulty' in Pynchon's work.

A more thoughtful and informative essay on Pynchon appeared in the *Cornell Alumni News* (November 1978) by Charles Hollander (who, incidentally, maintains that he has never met Pynchon). Noting Pynchon's continuing interest in the 'disinherited' of all kinds, Hollander states:

> Actually Pynchon does feel somewhat disinherited. Pynchon's family is a clan of bluebloods who were misguided enough to align themselves with the wrong side during not one, but two, American revolutions, one in the eighteenth century and one in the twentieth century, and who have suffered social and economic reversals as a consequence.

He notes that in Water's *Genealogical Gleanings* (London, 1901) it is stated that from William Pynchon's son John (that is the William Pynchon who brought his family to America in 1630) 'are descended all who bear that name in America'. On the basis of further research, Hollander says that one of those descendants, Joseph Pynchon, 'was groomed to become governor of Connecticut and would have been had he not been loyal to the Crown'. A Pynchon on the 'wrong' side, just as William Pynchon had alienated himself from the ruling Puritans by writing *The Meritorious Price of our Redemption*.

Hollander then moves to more recent times. Apparently there was a prominent stock-brokerage called Pynchon and Co. operating in the 1920s and 1930s. Given the range of Thomas Pynchon's interests, it is worth noting that this firm published pamphlets concerning topics that might interest potential investors – for instance, 'The Aviation Industry', 'Survey of Public Utilities', 'The Gas Industry' and 'Electric Light and Power: A Study of World Development' (this one in 1930). Is it by chance that Pynchon is, to my knowledge, the only writer ever to write the 'biography' of a light bulb (in *Gravity's Rainbow*)? Be that as it may, the Pynchon firm was one of the largest and most influential in America – if not the world (adds Hollander). Its reversals started after Black Thursday – the great stockmarket crash of 24 October 1929. 'By April 1931 the firm was suspended from the New York Stock Exchange and went into receivership.' It was, apparently, 'the largest brokerage ever to have been suspended from the NYSE'. Subsequently the Pynchon estate was sold and – Hollander comments – 'no end to ignominy, the estate's furniture was sold at public auction. Some reversal – from contemplating the world's electric power needs, to having the furniture sold at auction.' The firm had, apparently, been associated with the J. P. Morgan group: 'as the J. P. Morgan influence ebbed, the Morgan associates suffered as well. Once again the Pynchon clan had thrown its lot in with the loyalists and lost.'

Whatever importance one may choose to attach to all this, there is no doubt that Pynchon's works evince a great interest in, and sympathy with, 'losers' of all kinds. And it is true, as Hollander states, that in his early short fiction Pynchon 'seems more explicitly interested in the victims of the Great

Depression, which he hardly ever mentions in his novels, and their secret plans for return'. In 'The Secret Integration', for instance, there is the speculation that the hoboes who ride on freight trains are someone's 'relatives' who disappeared during the Great Depression. But the Depression does not entirely disappear from his longer fiction. Consider this from V. – remembering that Pynchon was born in 1937.

> On the way downtown on the subway he decided that we suffer from great temporal homesickness for the decade we were born in. Because he felt now as if he were living in some private depression days. . . . All around him were people in new suits, millions of inanimate objects being produced brand-new every week, new cars in the streets, houses going up by the thousands all over the suburbs he had left months ago. Where was the depression? In the sphere of Benny Profane's guts and in the sphere of his skull, concealed optimistically by a tight blue serge coat and a schlemihl's hopeful face. (p. 147)

America may seem or pretend to have forgotten the Depression, but Pynchon has not, and he knows that America really has not. Underneath all those proliferating 'brand-new' objects, the 'depression' has moved inside – and spread.

This is perhaps enough of a 'biographical' note. If Thomas Pynchon, author, has 'died' to the public, he has 'bequeathed' us his incomparable texts – and I hope he will give us more. His 'disappearance' is not only to be respected, but to be honoured, even applauded. Of course, the speculations continue. I conclude with one that had quite wide currency at one time: namely, that since, as it happens, the emergence of this new writer Thomas Pynchon coincided with the disappearance and (effectively) the silence of J. D. Salinger – well, Pynchon *was* Salinger simply using another name. This idea – or wild hypothesis – was published in an American journal called the *Soho Weekly News*. Pynchon responded with what one takes to be a wry, amused comment: 'Not bad, keep trying.' No doubt they will; but our concern is with the works in which we encounter, not Pynchon the individual author, but what Barthes calles the author's 'power to mix writings, to counter the ones with the others, in such a way as never to rest on any of them'. It is my contention, and belief, that no other living writer

(I'd better say in the English-speaking world) has 'mixed writings' to greater effect than Thomas Pynchon – whoever and wherever he is.

2

EARLY SHORT FICTION

Before considering Pynchon's early short fiction I want to make some general remarks concerning two phenomena – 'rubbish' and 'codes'. Any reader of Pynchon will recognize that he has an extraordinary feeling for what society designates as 'rubbish'. No one can write so lyrically or elegiacally about, for example, a second-hand car lot, or an old mattress, than Pynchon; and what other writer, in the course of a long and moving passage about Advent during wartime, would consider embarking on a curiously poignant meditation triggered off by thinking about 'thousands of old used toothpaste tubes' (*Gravity's Rainbow*, p. 130)? Many actual rubbish heaps or tips appear in his work – not as symbolic wastelands (though those are there too), but exactly as 'rubbish'. By extension, his work is populated by many of the categories (or non-categories) of people whom society regards as 'rubbish', socially useless junk: bums, hoboes, drifters, transients, itinerants, vagrants, the disinherited, the disaffected, derelicts, losers, victims. Pynchon is continually bringing such figures back from the relative invisibility to which society consigns them.

In this connection I want to introduce some statements made by Michael Thompson in his book, *Rubbish Theory*. Portions of the book can be faulted, but Thompson has a clear grasp of a point of central importance in Pynchon – namely, that what we regard as valuable and what we regard as rubbish are culturally determined.

> For the social order to be maintained there has to be some measure of agreement as to what is of value. People in different cultures may value different things, and they may

value the same things differently, but all cultures insist upon some distinction between the valued and the valueless.[5]

Thompson stresses that certain ways of discussing and categorizing things and people in society inevitably leave out some things (and people), literally overlooking them:

> serious adult thought in general, and sociology in particular, constitute a form of discourse that, of its very nature, is unable to make contact with certain regions of social life and, more important, . . . what goes in those regions is crucial for any understanding of society.[6]

Pynchon would, I think, agree. He is the great writer of the overlooked, the left-out, and thus offers a challenge to our often unexamined assumptions about the valuable and the valueless, the estimable and the dismissible. And, as Thompson notes, society's value-categories are intimately connected with questions of power: 'the manner in which durability and transience are imposed upon the world of objects' is related to 'the control mechanism within the system'. At the simplest level, yesterday's kitsch may become today's valuable antiques. This need not be solely due to the manipulation of those who control the market, but those in positions of power in that particular market can have a lot of influence over which category an object will be placed in. On a larger scale, society has a similar power over people. To use Thompson's words:

> only if one remains within severe cultural and temporal confines can one sustain the commonsense belief that rubbish is defined by intrinsic physical properties. Step outside these limits and one sees that the boundary between rubbish and non-rubbish moves in response to social pressures.[7]

Among other things, Pynchon's work is constantly taking the reader outside the limits of his 'cultural and temporal confines'.

Values and valuations are not, of course, fixed. Society may withdraw as well as confer 'value': it is one of the ways in which societies change. Pynchon, like any great writer, makes us re-examine the dominant valuations of our age. His work is a counterforce to what Thompson designates as two kinds of blindness:

> there are those things or areas which we cannot see (though those with an entirely different 'game' may be able to see

21

them), and there are those things or areas which we conspire not to see. When these latter intrude, and we cannot help but see them, we banish them from view (or, alternatively, neutralize their visibility) by assigning them to a unique cross-cultural category which may be labelled 'rubbish'.[8]

Pynchon indeed plays a different 'game' and is constantly exposing the conspiracy of 'invisibility', that hidden social collusion – a kind of 'plot' – which decides and decrees what is valuable and what is 'rubbish'.

Having introduced the word 'plot', I can move on to make some general remarks about 'codes'. Pynchon's work is full of plots and codes – at every level, from political plots, spies, conspiracies and all kinds of private forms of communication, to larger, national, global, even metaphysical and religious questions concerning the possible presence or absence of plots, and more mystical kinds of illumination or 'messages' or communication (or 'communion', an important word for Pynchon) than the ciphers of espionage or the code of a secret society. Some precedent for this interest can be found in earlier American literature, most notably in the work of Poe. In his work there is not really any presence of 'nature' as one finds it in, say, Fenimore Cooper, but rather a series of cryptograms or clues which have to be decoded, interpreted, translated. The reader of Poe has to be a kind of detective (he, of course, effectively invented the detective story) and a cryptographer. This is true of Pynchon's readers – and many of his characters. In an essay entitled 'A Few Words on Secret Writing' Poe wrote:

> as we can scarcely imagine a time when there did not exist a necessity, or at least a desire, of transmitting information from one individual to another in such a manner as to elude general comprehension, so we may well suppose the practice of writing in cipher to be of great antiquity.[9]

That 'necessity' or 'desire' is notably present in Pynchon's work. It is not, however, a simple matter of cracking a code. Nor is it in Poe. For example, in chapter 23 of *The Narrative of Arthur Gordon Pym* the topography of a strange island is described. At one point the two men exploring the island find a series of 'indentures in the surface', but these are equivocal.

22

With a very slight exertion of the imagination, the left, or more northerly of these indentures might have been taken for the intentional, though rude, representation of a human figure . . . the rest of them bore also some little resemblance to alphabetical characters, and Peters was willing, in all events, to adopt the idle opinion that they were really such.

Pym, on the other hand, is convinced that they are 'the work of nature'. Does nature have its own language of signs, or do we 'alphabetize' nature in looking at it?

The problem becomes a dominant one in Pynchon, where figures like Stencil in *V.* and Oedipa Maas in *Lot 49* have to try to work out whether they really are discovering clues, finding codes and seeing signs, or whether they are projecting or hallucinating in a plotless, clueless world. And, as we shall see, it is often in so-called 'rubbish' that they have to engage in their ambiguous quest for signs. The following quotation gives some sense of Pynchon's feeling for what we might call the esoteric message which may be concealed by the exoteric message, subtexts legible only to the initiated. Pynchon is referring to a secret society of those who have been struck by lightning (the enlightened?):

> Between congruent and identical there seems to be another class of look-alike that only finds the lightning-heads. Another world laid down on the previous one and to all appearances no different. Ha-*ha*! But the lightning-struck know, all right! . . . [they receive a] private monthly magazine *A Nickel Saved* (which looks perfectly innocent, old Ben Franklin after inflation, unless you know the other half of the proverb: '. . . is a stockpile of nickel'. Making the *real* quote nickel-magnate Mark Hanna's 'You have been in politics long enough to know that no man in public office owes the public anything.' So the real title is *Long Enough*, which Those Who Know, know. The text of each issue of the magazine, when transformed this way, yields many interesting messages). To outsiders it's just a pleasant little club newsletter . . . (*Gravity's Rainbow*, pp. 664–5)

We can read Pynchon like 'outsiders', or like the lightning-struck. But Those Who Know, know.

Pynchon's first published story was 'The Small Rain' (*The*

Cornell Writer, 6 (March 1959)). There are already clearly discernible types, themes, even atmospheres, which he will develop in subsequent work. The main figure is Nathan Levine, who has deliberately enlisted in the army. He is stationed at some desolate piece of nowhere in Louisiana which he actually likes. He likes the inertia, the inaction, the repetition, the not having to think (he is a graduate from CCNY), and the not having to feel. This cherished immunity from feeling is to be a dominant and recurring phenomenon in Pynchon's work. He is also, paradoxically enough, a communications expert. However, his unit is suddenly ordered into action when a hurricane devastates the bayou country of southern Louisiana. Although Levine likes most of all to 'sleep' or drift off into pornographic novels – notably, one called *Swamp Wench* – the disaster stirs him into some kind of action and change. 'He was also starting to worry: to anticipate some radical change, perhaps, after three years of sand, concrete and sun.' This emergence into a degree of wakefulness and activity is provoked by two things: the disaster, and the hundreds of hideous corpses that have to be dragged from the water; and the college kids on the campus where they have been stationed. There is not only perpetual rain but the air is full of the smell of death. Levine begins to see the horror and the reality of it. He also sees how cut-off from it all the college kids are, 'each trying to look at it as something unusual and nothing they had ever been or would ever want ever to be part of.' Levine has a vision of a kind of life – or death-in-life – which is

> something like a closed circuit. Everybody on the same frequency. And after a while you forget about the rest of the spectrum and start believing that this is the only frequency that counts or is real. While outside, all up and down the land, there are these wonderful colors and x-rays and ultraviolets going on.

Too many people in Pynchon's world try to prolong life as 'a closed circuit' in some way or another, so that they can 'forget about the rest'. On impulse – it is not his official job – Levine joins the men on one of the tugs who are picking up the dead bodies. It is a wasteland indeed – 'gray sun on gray swamp' – the rain not bringing fertility and new life, but death. The point is that Levine at least makes the gesture of doing something.

'Levine worked in silence like the others . . . realizing somehow that the situation did not require thought or rationalization. He was picking up stiffs. That was what he was doing.' It is as though the actual vision of – and contact with – death has brought him out of his anaesthetized and paralysed state. Not, of course, that he can do much about the situation, nor does he experience any miraculous transformation. But he acted, and it seems to indicate that he cannot go back into his old state. Instead, he sees himself living the life of a wanderer.

> He had a momentary, ludicrous vision of himself, Lardass Levine the Wandering Jew, debating on weekday evenings in strange and nameless towns with other Wandering Jews the essential problems of identity – not of the self so much as an identity of place and what right you really had to be anyplace.

We do not see his future, but just such displaced wanderers will roam through Pynchon's later fiction.

Near the end Levine picks up a coed who calls herself 'little Buttercup'. For a night in a cabin in a nearby swamp she is, indeed, his 'swamp wench'. Partly because his attitude towards women appears to be basically pornographic, and partly because of the girl's 'incapacity to give', there is no love, no human contact at all, in the coupling. Afterwards, Levine says 'In the midst of great death, the little death.' Doubtless he intends a pun (death as sexual climax), but it points to a larger truth: that what should be the act of love has been turned into an act of death. This deformation of sex into death – or the substitution of death for love – is one of the modern malaises to which Pynchon returns and which he analyses in his longer fiction. When Levine leaves the area, it is still raining, and he says to a friend, 'Jesus Christ I hate rain.' His friend answers, 'You and Hemingway. Funny, ain't it. T. S. Eliot likes rain.' This may be seen as a rejection of Eliot's values or poetic stance, though Levine is no Hemingway. Still, he has been shaken out of his nonchalance, that cultivated non-identity or emotional anonymity of the 'enlisted man'; he has lost some of his immunity from feeling. Although we last see him asleep (again), he cannot, we feel, ever go 'back' to the inert condition he was in at the start, living like a 'closed circuit', and forgetting all the rest.

Pynchon's next story was 'Mortality and Mercy in Vienna' (published in *Epoch*, 9 (Spring 1959)). Summarized very reductively, it can be described as an account of a party in Washington (the first of many such parties in Pynchon's work which invariably degenerate into violence and chaos), at the end of which, we infer, a strange Indian from Ontario (Irving Loon) starts to massacre all the guests prior, again we infer, to eating them. Stated thus baldly, the idea of the story might seem to be just a piece of sick – very sick – humour. But into this remarkable story Pynchon has packed a number of very suggestive notions which are important in relation to his later work. We can start with the title, which comes from *Measure for Measure*. When the Duke, Vincentio, effectively 'abdicates' in the first scene, he hands over all his ducal power to Angelo:

> In our remove be thou at full ourself;
> Mortality and mercy in Vienna
> Live in thy tongue and heart.

The theme of self-removal and substitution of authority is central to Pynchon's story, in which Washington is depicted as being as degenerate and corrupt as the Vienna in Shakespeare's play, and in which a hugely disproportionate 'justice' is meted out to the errant and debauched guests, just as the death penalty imposed upon Claudio is quite incommensurable with his sin or crime of making Julietta ('fast my wife') pregnant. The problem, in both works, is how do you – can you, can anyone? – cure or heal a degenerate and, as it were, 'damned' society? In Shakespeare's play, Escalus offers a kind of pragmatic doctoring, Angelo a would-be Messianic healing which is both hypocritical and inhuman, and the Duke a type of apocalyptic judgement which is truly just, therapeutic – and merciful.

Pynchon's story also starts with an abdication and a substitution. The main figure, Cleanth Siegel, a junior diplomat, arrives at a party only to find that his original host, Rachel, will not be there. Instead he finds a somewhat crazed man, David Lupescu, whom Siegel half recognizes as a *Doppelgänger* and who instantly seizes on Siegel as 'Mon semblable . . . mon frère' and also 'a sign, a deliverance'. He hands over responsibility for the party to Siegel with words that are loaded with religious resonance. 'It's all yours. You are now the host. As host you are a trinity: (a) receiver of guests . . . (b) an enemy and (c) an outward manifestation, for *them*, of the divine body and blood.' As he leaves, Siegel asks him where he is going, and Lupescu answers in words that deliberately invoke Conrad's *Heart of Darkness*. 'The outside . . . out of the jungle . . . Mistah Kurtz – he dead.' So by a use of literary reference or intertextuality, a device that Pynchon makes more use of than any other living writer – mixing writings, in Barthes's words – the Washington party is not only Shakespeare's Vienna but also Conrad's jungle (with a trace of Baudelaire's particular Paris). One question will be: how will Siegel act as the designated and chosen substitute 'host'? Like the Duke, or Angelo; like Marlow or Kurtz? Will he be a true host – or go crazy?

The question is quite central to Pynchon's work, so I shall go into it in a little more detail. Siegel is a mixed figure. His mother is a Catholic and he grows up religious, until he gives up his faith (at college he is known as Stephen – a nod at Joyce). But he retains inside him 'the still small Jesuit voice'. On the other hand there is a 'nimble little Machiavel' inside him who not only enjoys 'scheming and counterscheming' and 'manipulating campus opinion' but is also – as Machiavelli advised – capable of delegating cruel actions to others. (Machiavelli is an important figure in Pynchon's work.) He is, then, as one of his college friends murmurs, a 'House divided against itself', the reference here, of course, being to Christ's words in Mark 3:24–6:

> How can Satan drive out Satan? If a kingdom is divided against itself, that kingdom cannot stand; if a household is divided against itself, that house will never stand: and if Satan is in rebellion against himself, he is divided and cannot stand: and that is the end of him.

As we discover, Siegel, finally, 'cannot stand'. When he was younger he had regarded himself as 'a kind of healer . . . a prophet actually, because if you cared about it at all you had to be both', though he was worried that one could easily become 'something less – a doctor, or a fortune-teller'. The possibility of any real healing and prophecy recurs throughout Pynchon. More generally, the problem becomes nothing less than how to be in the contemporary world, particularly if it is as infernal as the Washington party implies. One way is to cultivate disengagement, emotional immunity: keeping 'cool', to use a term deployed by Pynchon. But that, of course, can lead to paralysis and inhumanity. The other extreme is to want to be a great healer and prophet, but that can lead to a different kind of inhumanity – and madness (Kurtz). Pynchon's work is constantly seeking to discover something in between these two extremes.

In Siegel's case at the party he goes through different phases. He acts as a 'father confessor' to a number of 'the whole host of trodden-on and disaffected': he looks 'compassionate' and listens while people expose to him 'synapses and convolutions which should never have been exposed . . . the bad lands of the heart'. In his way he gives them 'absolution or penance, but no practical advice'. (Kurtz's eloquence contained no 'practical hints'; Marlow is more pragmatic.) But for a time he does attempt positive, practical, restorative work: 'This little Jesuit thing, this poltergeist, would start kicking around inside his head . . . and call him back to the real country where there were drinks to be mixed and *bon mots* to be tossed out carelessly and maybe a drunk or two to take care of.' This proto-religious instinct to 'take care' of people is supplemented by his 'true British staff-officer style to bite the jolly old bullet and make the best of a bad job'. But then he gets 'fed up' with the role he feels has been imposed upon him: 'It was a slow process and dangerous because in the course of things it was very possible to destroy not only yourself but your flock as well.' He starts to disengage himself.

The crisis is precipitated by the Indian, Loon (lunatic). Siegel remembers hearing about his tribe, the Ojibwa Indians, in an anthropology course. Because of their bleak and austere way of life, living always on the brink of starvation, this tribe is prone to 'psychopathy' and 'saturated with anxiety'. The Ojibwa hunter characteristically experiences a 'vision' after which

> he feels he has acquired a supernatural companion, and there is a tendency to identify . . . [for] the Ojibwa hunter, feeling as he does at bay, feeling a concentration of obscure cosmic forces against him and him alone, cynical terrorists, savage and amoral deities which are bent on his destruction, the identification may become complete.

This feeling or state of mind is one experienced by many

subsequent figures in Pynchon's work. And, most importantly perhaps, these Indians have strong 'paranoid tendencies' – the first time the word 'paranoid' appears in Pynchon, but 'paranoia' is to become one of his central concerns. In the case of the Ojibwa their paranoia can lead to the 'Windigo psychosis', which, briefly, leads them to identify with a supernatural figure – the Windigo – who eats people, thus turning them into 'frenzied cannibals' who first 'gorge' themselves on their 'immediate family' and then start to devour people at random. From certain signs Siegel realizes that Irving Loon is very close to the 'Windigo psychosis' and is thus about to erupt into devastating violence and cannibalism. This does indeed bring the 'Moment of truth' for Siegel.

If he has read the signs correctly, 'Siegel has the power to work for these parishioners a kind of miracle, to bring them a very tangible salvation. A miracle involving a host, true, but like no holy eucharist.' He has it in his power to 'save' the whole group; but he has lost his concern with them, thinking he 'should tell all these people to go to hell'. In effect he sends them there. He suddenly sees Irving Loon starting to load a rifle and realizes that the massacre is about to start. Siegel is 'paralyzed'. Then, realizing he has 'about sixty seconds to make a decision', the different parts of the house divided against itself – the Machiavel, the Jesuit, the gentle part, the 'John Buchan hero' part – agree that there is really only one course to take; 'it was just unfortunate that Irving Loon would be the only one partaking of any body and blood, divine or otherwise'. He issues no saving warnings but simply walks away, encased in a chilling indifference. As he hears the first screams and shots, 'He shrugged. What the hell, stranger things had happened in Washington.' Such insouciant callousness is a terrible sign of man's ability to dehumanize himself. Siegel has indeed allowed his 'flock' to be 'destroyed', and in the process he has destroyed himself – as a human being – as well. Satan cannot drive out Satan; and that is the end of him. Irving Siegel is not just an example of a failed healer, a false prophet. He is both a product and a representative of a society that has accepted – indeed, eagerly embraced – 'mortality' on an ever-increasing scale, and has forgotten the 'mercy'.

'Low Lands' followed in 1960 (*New World Writing*, 16). In strict narrative terms it is about a lawyer named Dennis Flange who one day decides not to go to work so that he can drink with the garbage man, Rocco Squarcione. They are joined by an old navy friend of Flange, a gross figure named Pig Bodine (who recurs in later work). This is too much for Flange's wife Cindy and she orders them all out of the house. Rocco takes the others in his truck to a large garbage dump – vividly evoked by Pynchon, as we might expect – and introduces them to Bolingbroke, the watchman and 'king' of the dump. He puts them up for the night in his shack after they have told sea stories. Flange is awakened by a call from a girl who turns out to be a midget gypsy named Nerissa, who is convinced she will marry an 'Anglo'. She leads him by secret tunnels to her underground room. The story concludes with his agreeing to stay with her – at least for a while. The story takes place on three different levels: Flange's house above the sea; the dump at sea level; the subterranean complex of secret tunnels. Each has a different kind of residence: Flange's house was a minister's house from the 1920s; then there is the watchman's shack; finally Nerissa's room underground. There are connections: the house is full of secret tunnels associated with the smuggling that went on in the twenties, in which the minister was involved and to which he took a 'romantic attitude'; these are echoed by the network of underground tunnels beneath the dump, constructed in the thirties by a terrorist group called 'the Sons of the Red Apocalypse', and in the present time of the story occupied by gypsies.

As the story progresses, Flange moves further away from his wife, and further away from established society, first to the company of nonconformists and social derelicts, then yet further away to the gypsies – socially completely ostracized, 'rubbish' in social terms, and only able to 'live' by night. For 'further away' we could read 'deeper away', since for Flange the action is a continual descent. The house is up, the dump is down ('It seemed to Flange that they must be heading for the centre of the spiral, the low point') and the gypsy's room yet further down ('He had not realized that the junk pile ran to such a depth'). In every case, going from room to room Flange is going from womb to womb – as he knows – and perhaps prior to some regeneration and redemption (the ending leaves it deliberately equivocal; it might also be a descent into fantasy or even insanity). But a descent it is (Flange's 'Molemanship' is referred to), through varying strata of society's 'rubbish' (starting with the established society itself), and Flange is indeed burrowing. He is also drawn to the sea: 'he had read or heard somewhere in his pre-adolescence that the sea was a woman and the metaphor had enslaved him and largely determined what he became from that moment.' At times he also sees the sea as a 'waste land which stretches away to the horizon'. Nerissa the midget is a kind of mermaid of the dump. Flange's 'drowning' in the dump may make possible a sea change in his life, in his conception of the world. Just before he is summoned by Nerissa he falls asleep misquoting *The Tempest* and wondering whether he has perhaps 'suffered a sea change into something not so rare or strange'.

This leads us to another aspect of the whole story: among other things it is a tissue of references, allusions, quotations and misquotations, ironic echoes and parodies – mixed writings. Writers and works thus evoked in some way include T. S. Eliot (with a light travesty of the Waste Land myth), Shakespeare's *The Tempest, Henry IV* (Bolingbroke, of course), *The Merchant of Venice* (Nerissa is Portia's maid), *Alice's Adventures in Wonderland, Keats's Endymion*. More distinctly the story is a clear echo, and rewriting, of Washington Irving's story – so crucial for American literature – 'Rip Van Winkle'. In all this mixing of writings and rewritings, Pynchon is not simply amusing himself or winking at learned readers. We should see this activity – which continues throughout his major works – more as a sifting (or 'burrowing' back) through not exactly the 'rubbish' and 'waste' of our literary past but through its accumulations to see what can be re-used (recycled, perhaps) for depicting his particular fictional world. We do not have to identify the other texts, but we do have to be alert for clues. Alert on all sides – noting, for example, that the 1920s are associated with the irresponsible 'romanticism' of the minister's house, while the 1930s saw the founding of 'the terrorist group called the Sons of the Red Apocalypse' when the whole social and political climate had changed. Pynchon is, among other things, a notable historical novelist, as *Gravity's Rainbow* was supremely to reveal. And again he can see that neither of the two suggested ways of being in – or against – society, worked or can work: the delusions of romanticism are matched by the delusions of apocalyptic revolutionary politics (they both used 'tunnels', but society still stood).

31

The story concludes with the beginning of the emergence of a new attitude in Flange, whether it is 'dream' or genuine transformation. Earlier we had read that he had a recurring dread of shrinkage – of himself, and of the world:

> What he worried about was any eventual convexity, a shrinking, it might be, of the planet itself to some palpable curvature of whatever he would be standing on, so that he would be left sticking out like a projected radius, unsheltered and reeling across the empty lunes of his tiny sphere.

At the end, in Nerissa's room, he has a different attitude. And it is important to note that to Flange she looks like a child (just as her pet rat looks like her child): children are always a source of value in Pynchon and attitudes to them always indicative of something positive or negative in an adult. The story ends:

> And then: I wonder why Cindy and I never had a child.
> And: a child makes it all right. Let the world shrink to a *boccie* ball.
> So of course he knew.
> 'Sure' he said. 'All right. I'll stay.' For a while, at least, he thought. She looked up gravely. Whitecaps danced across her eyes; sea creatures, he knew, would be cruising about in the submarine green of her heart.

So of course *we* do *not* know – except that something is happening to Flange, and that Pynchon has produced a text that is rare and strange, ranging through many moods and tones, dense with resonances and implications, and ending at an equivocal suspended moment which has a haunting beauty all its own.

'Entropy' was published in 1960 (*Kenyon Review*, 22). It is composed like a fugue, and relevant words like 'stretto', 'counterpoint' and 'fugue' occur in the text. The 'counterpoint' is mainly between two floors of a Washington apartment building. Downstairs one Meatball Mulligan is having a 'lease-breaking party' which seems to be degenerating into chaos. Upstairs a figure named Callisto and his girlfriend Aubade live in a curious fantasy room: a 'hothouse jungle it had taken him seven years to weave together. Hermetically sealed, it was a tiny enclave of regularity in the city's chaos, alien to the vagaries of the weather, of national politics, of any civil disorder.' 'They did not go out.' Outside there is rain and it is the season of the 'false spring'. Two notable conversations take place in the growing din of the party. One concerns communication theory.

Tell a girl: 'I love you'. No trouble with two-thirds of that, it's a closed circuit. Just you and she. But that nasty four-letter word in the middle *that's* the one you have to look out for. Ambiguity. Redundance. Irrelevance, even. Leakage. All this is noise. Noise screws up your signal, makes for disorganization in the circuit.

Upstairs Callisto and Aubade have indeed created a 'closed circuit', just he and she. But such hermetically maintained order is a form of death. Noise indeed 'screws up your signal', but this might have a potential value if you want to cause 'disorganization in the circuit'. This, I think, can apply to Pynchon's work, which does indeed make for 'disorganization' in the customary circuits. So we must be prepared for 'Ambiguity. Redundance. Irrelevance, even. Leakage.' They may be the condition for the emergence of new kinds of signal. On the other hand, as Pynchon's story indicates, total noise – total chaos – would mean just no communication at all.

This problem is made clear in another form in the other conversation I wish to mention. There is a jazz quartet at the party and after pushing experimentation to the limit – there are distinct echoes of Gerry Mulligan and Ornette Coleman – they finally 'play' a completely silent piece, using no instruments. As the group's leader, the Duke, admits, the next logical extension 'is to think everything'. And thus to pass beyond music – and communication – altogether. The Duke says that they still have some problems, and Meatball says 'Back to the old drawing board.' ' "No, man," Duke said, "back to the airless void." ' Again this reflects on Pynchon's own position as a writer seeking some radically new form of fictional 'music'. He does not want to go back to 'the old drawing board'; but he knows that the 'airless void' is a place where no messages – no music – can take place at all.

An 'airless void' is something like what Callisto and Aubade have created in their 'hothouse' refuge. It is a deliberate retreat from the world. Drawing on Henry Adams and Gibbs, Callisto outlines his preoccupation with 'entropy' (an idea used not only in thermodynamics but in information theory); like Adams, Callisto speaks of himself in the third person:

he found in entropy or the measure of disorganization for a closed system an adequate metaphor to apply to certain phenomena in his own world . . . in American 'consumerism' discovered a similar tendency from the least to the most probable, from differentiation to sameness, from ordered individuality to a kind of chaos. He found himself, in short, restating Gibbs' prediction in social terms, and envisioned a heat-death for his culture in which ideas, like heat-energy, would no longer be transferred since each point in it would ultimately have the same quantity of energy; and intellectual motion would, accordingly, cease.

As he talks, he is trying to save the life of a young bird by warming it in his hands – transferring heat – but he finally fails, since he has indeed brought about an entropic state in his 'closed system'. What frightens him is that the temperature outside has remained at 37 degrees Fahrenheit for some days, and he takes this as an 'omen of apocalypse'. But while the idea of entropy is very important in Pynchon's work we should note that it is metaphor embraced, not by the author, but by the self-isolated Callisto. (It is worth noting that at one point he is looking for 'correspondences' and he thinks of Sade, and what happens to Temple Drake in *Sanctuary*, and *Nightwood* – all works or authors alluding to acts of sexual perversion.)

While it might seem that there is a simple opposition between the accelerating chaos downstairs and the calm upstairs ('arabesques of order competing fugally with the improvised discords of the party downstairs'), it is not, of course, so simple – as the conclusion intimates. Mulligan finds himself confronting a somewhat similar choice to that which confronted Siegel and confronts many other figures in Pynchon: give up, or try to do something?

The way he figured, there were only two ways he could cope: (a) lock himself in the closet and maybe eventually they would all go away, or (b) try to calm everybody down, one by one. (a) was certainly the more attractive alternative. But then he started thinking about that closet. It was dark and stuffy and he would be alone. . . . The other way was more a pain in the neck, but probably better in the long run. So he decided to try and keep his lease-breaking party from deteriorating into total chaos . . .

It might not be a radical solution, but it is a gesture against chaos, a neg-entropic act; while upstairs the girl Aubade finally breaks the window of their hothouse with her bare hands

and turned to face the man on the bed and wait with him until the moment of equilibrium was reached, when 37 degrees Fahrenheit should prevail both outside and inside, and forever, and the hovering, curious dominant of their separate lives should resolve into a tonic of darkness and the final absence of all motion.

There is a kind of perfect music which acts like a 'closed system' and finally resolves all into a terminal sameness: there is a noise which might indeed lead to chaos (a terminal sameness of another kind) but which might also permit new signals and provoke some counterforce against chaos, against terminal sameness – against entropy. The attractions of 'the closet' in the madness of the modern world are clear enough in Pynchon, but so is the need to resist those attractions in some way. The 'closed circuit', the sealed-off refuge, the hothouse world of fantasy, the dangerous seductiveness of metaphors of doom (like entropy): these can all lead to inhumanity and death. Pynchon, the writer, moves and manœuvres between the 'old drawing board' and the 'airless void'.

'Under the Rose' (*Noble Savage*, 3 (1961)) was later re-worked as chapter 3 in *V.*, but a few points should be noted about the story, since it revealed for the first time another dimension of Pynchon's imagination: his ability to reconstruct history for his own purposes (the astonishing range of this reconstructive gift was only to emerge fully in *Gravity's Rainbow*). It is set at the time of the Fashoda Crisis of 1898. This was the climax of a series of conflicts between Great Britain and France, and although it resulted in the *entente* of 1904 it revealed the possible dangers of the international conflicts always latent in the period of late imperialism, and it could be seen, retrospectively, as an omen of the First World War. Fashoda was the strategic centre of the Egyptian Sudan, land of the Upper Nile, and both the British (under Kitchener) and the French (under Marchand) engaged in a race to capture it – forces converging on a single point (as they will on Malta in *V.*).

National feelings ran so high that it did indeed bring the countries to the brink of war.

Pynchon's story is concerned with the spying that went on in the background – 'spying's Free Masonry' – and the sense of the approach of some 'sure apocalypse'. One German spy longs for a big, final war, an Armageddon. The English spy, Porpentine, has 'conceived the private mission of keeping off Armageddon'. But they are both 'comrade Machiavellians, still playing the games of the Renaissance'. All the spies operate 'in no conceivable Europe but rather in a zone forsaken by God, between the tropics of diplomacy, lines they were forbidden forever to cross'. A similar 'zone' is to reappear in *Gravity's Rainbow*. One spy looks forward to the possible great war as effecting a great 'cleaning': 'Armageddon would sweep the house of Europe so. Did that make Porpentine champion only of cobwebs, rubbish, offscourings?' And Pynchon, too? Porpentine is another of those Pynchon figures concerned with the problems of being a 'saviour'.

> Porpentine found it necessary to believe if one appointed oneself saviour of humanity that perhaps one must love that humanity only in the abstract. For any descent to the personal level can make a purpose less pure. Whereas a disgust at individual human perversity might as easily avalanche into a rage for apocalypse.

There are references to an increasing inclination to turn to the 'inanimate' (a girl 'daft for rocks', a man who has himself wired up so that he can operate like a machine), a dominant motif in *V*.. Porpentine, old-fashioned, crosses a 'threshold' into 'humanity': it is fatal, and the story ends up with his death. The larger question posed – if there is a larger question than the problem of being 'human' in the modern world – is one that hangs over all Pynchon's subsequent work.

> It was no longer single combat. Had it ever been? . . . They were all in it; all had a stake, acted as a unit. Under orders. Whose orders? Anything human? He doubted . . . excused himself, silent, for wanting so to believe in a fight according to the duello, even in this period of history. But they – no, it – had not been playing those rules. Only statistical odds. When had he stopped facing an adversary and taken on a Force, a Quantity?

36

All the 'rules' of an earlier world have gone. There is now only a 'they'. Or, rather, an 'it'. We are entering the modern world.

Two more short pieces by Pynchon may conveniently be mentioned here, although they were written after the publication of *V.*. 'The Secret Integration' (*Saturday Evening Post*, 237 (19 December 1964)) concerns a group of boys led by Grover Snodd who indulge in various attempts at sabotaging the local paper mill or the school – an undertaking named Operation Spartacus (after the film). Most of them are childish adventure games, and as 'plots' they fail when it comes to the lines of authority laid down by the adult world, though there is some anarchic resentment against 'the sealed-up world adults made, remade and lived in without him'. The title refers to the events that follow the moving of a black family, the Barringtons, into the town of Mingeborough: the white adults are all bigots and behave hysterically at the presence of the black family in their community. Among other things, they cover the front lawn of the Barrington house with garbage. When the gang of boys discover this – and the gang includes the black boy Carl Barrington – they 'begin kicking through it looking for clues'. (Looking for clues in garbage is a recurrent activity in Pynchon!) The clues they find reveal that a good deal of the garbage comes from their own homes. Through shame or feelings of helplessness they effectively abandon Carl, and he drifts away into the darkness, off to the old derelict mansion which is their secret hideout. Carl is in every sense a reject, and constructed out of rejections – indeed, we finally discover that he is an 'imaginary playmate'.

> Carl has been put together out of phrases, images, possibilities that grownups had somehow turned away from, repudiated, left out at the edges of the town, as if they were auto parts in Etienne's father's junkyard – things they could or did not want to live with but which the kids, on the other hand, could spend endless hours with, piecing together, rearranging, feeding, programming, refining. He was entirely theirs, their friend and robot, to cherish, buy undrunk sodas for, or send into danger or even, as now, at last, to banish from their sight.

So they leave their fantasy friend Carl and return 'each to his own house, hot shower, dry towel, before-bed television, good night kiss, and dreams that could never again be entirely safe'.

Another incident involves another black, a vagrant and a drifter named Mr McAfee. The children go to the hotel to try to help him (he is an alcoholic, and one of the children is already a member of Alcoholics Anonymous!). At one point the children try to telephone a girl the man once knew. This gives Tim an intimation of just what kind of terrifying loneliness is possible: 'Tim's foot felt at the edge of a certain abyss which he had been walking close to – for who knew how long – without knowing'; he sees 'how hard it would be, how hopeless, to really find a person you needed suddenly, unless you lived all your life in a house like he did, with a mother and father'. The white adults drive McAfee out of town next morning. Again, the children are really helpless. The town has certainly not accepted 'integration'. Tim asks his friend Grover, a maths prodigy, what the word 'integration' means:

> 'The opposite of differentiation,' Grover said, drawing an x-axis, y-axis and curve on his greenboard. 'Call this function of x. Consider values of the curve at any point little increments of x' – drawing straight vertical lines from the curve down to the x-axis, like the bars of a jail cell – 'you can have as many of these as you want, see, as close together as you want.'
> 'Till it's all solid,' said Tim.
> 'No, it never gets solid. If this was a jail cell, and those lines were bars, and whoever was behind it could make himself any size he wanted to be, he could always make himself skinny enough to get free. No matter how close together the bars were.'

Grover knows that the lines are artificial, but in fact in the adult world they do operate as cell bars, and instead of integration plus differentiation this white society will try to maintain a rigid and exclusive sameness, as solid as it can make it. The ultimate emptiness and deadness of such a society is manifest in the new housing estate as perceived by the children:

> But there was nothing about the little, low-rambling, more or less identical homes of Northumberland Estates to interest or to haunt . . . no small immunities, no possibilities for hidden life or otherworldly presence: no trees, secret

routes, shortcuts, culverts, thickets that could be made hollow in the middle – everything in the place was out in the open, everything could be seen at a glance; and behind it, under it, around the corners of its houses and down the safe, gentle curves of its streets, you came back you kept coming back, to nothing: nothing but the cheerless earth.

The end of the story sees the end of fantasy, of rebellion and perhaps of innocence, for the children have encountered the nasty realities of adult prejudice inside their own comfortable homes. But this kind of man-made landscape of 'nothing' becomes an increasing source of dread in Pynchon's work. Elsewhere and in different ways the rebellion against the 'sealed-up world adults made' goes on – and must go on.

Pynchon's one piece of journalism, 'A Journey into the Mind of Watts' (*New York Times Magazine*, 12 June 1966), was a study of the Los Angeles slums where the riots took place. Perhaps predictably, Pynchon is drawn to the Watts Towers, some towers made literally out of garbage by an Italian immigrant, Simon Rodia, who devoted his life to these weird constructions – 'his own dream of how things should have been: a fantasy of fountains, boats, tall openwork spires, encrusted with a dazzling mosaic of Watts debris.' Pynchon describes Los Angeles as 'a little unreal' because, 'more than any other city, [it] belongs to the mass media'. And Watts lies 'impacted at the heart of this white fantasy'. Pynchon describes how violence is inevitable in the circumstances. The people who live in Watts are among those disinherited for whom Pynchon has such a particular sympathy. He notes not only their actual poverty but the emptiness of their lives: 'Watts is full of street corners where people stand, as they have been, some of them, for 20 or 30 years, without Surprise One ever coming along.' Life without 'surprise' – the unpredictable, the random, 'difference' – is no life at all. It is also in keeping with Pynchon's imagination that he should end the piece on a proto-apocalyptic note. He describes an example of Watts art: 'it is a broken TV set, inside the cavity that once held the picture tube there is a human skull'. It is called: 'The Late, Late, Late Show'. And Pynchon knows what they meant by that.

3

'V.'

Pynchon's *V.* (1963), although it received a good deal of positive acclaim, has not been well served by the critics. '*V.* is like a riddle that, once correctly answered, never taxes the mind again': Robert Sklar's comment is not untypical. Even such a committed Pynchon enthusiast as Edward Mendelson, while invoking Joyce's *Ulysses* in passing, seems to see *V.* as simply the 'overgrown elaboration of a simple idea' – namely, 'the decline of the animate into the inanimate'. There is no doubt at all about the recurring presence of this idea; indeed, the word 'inanimate' occurs so often (five times on one page) that one may be inclined to wonder if it is much of a 'riddle' to solve, if indeed it is not so over-visible and over-stressed that perhaps something else is going on. Certainly a great deal is going on, and I cannot see that such reductive criticism does justice to the wealth of the novel.

It has been noted that we can find echoes, allusions to and parodies of many other genres and writers in it. Spy novels, adventure novels, historical and political novels, romantic and pornographic or perverted novels – all are invoked; and one can detect traces of Conrad, Lawrence Durrell, Evelyn Waugh, Melville, Henry Adams, Nathanael West, Djuna Barnes, Faulkner, Dashiell Hammett and many other writers, not to mention works like *The Golden Bough* and *The White Goddess*. But it is not merely a clever exercise in collage, any more than I can see it as fitting in the category of 'black humour' to which it has been assigned more than once. Pynchon is indeed offering us 'mixed writings' again, and on a vast scale, just as the book itself ranges historically from the end of the nineteenth century up to the present of the narrative, and geographically over a number of continents. In addition, Pynchon brings in a good deal of science, particularly physics and advanced technology, and the final effect is, to my mind, very far from being simple – just as the mood can change from one of near or actual farce (and Pynchon is among other things an extremely amusing writer) to one of elegiac sadness; from intimations of apocalypse to glimpses of pentecostal hope; from scenes of sustained horror to passages of sustained visionary intensity which make him truly one of the most poetic prose writers of our time. So instead of seeing the book as a riddle to be solved (and forgotten), or the excessive elaboration of a single theme, we might consider another way into the book.

I have noted that Pynchon's concerns are usually related in one way or another to problems of decipherment and what Lukács describes as 'the incommensurability of . . . interiority and adventure – in the absence of a transcendental "place" allotted to human endeavours', particularly as this incommensurability manifests itself in a permanent instability in the relationship between the interpreting mind and the varying fields of signification that it must negotiate. (See the chapter 'Abstract Idealism' in *The Theory of the Novel*.) Lukács designates two kinds of 'incommensurability': 'either the inner world is narrower or it is broader than the outside world assigned to it as the arena and substratum of its actions'.[10] Shortly after, Lukács engages in his own account of *Don Quixote*:

> the first great novel of world literature stands at the beginning of time when the Christian God began to forsake the world; when man became lonely and could find meaning and substance only in his own soul, whose home was nowhere; when the world, released from its paradoxical anchorage in a beyond that is truly present, was abandoned to its imminent meaninglessness; when the power of what is – reinforced by Utopian links, now degraded to mere existence – had grown to incredible magnitude and was waging a furious, apparently aimless struggle against the new forces which were as yet weak and incapable of revealing themselves or penetrating the world.[11]

These words are by no means inapplicable to *V.*, and I suggest that Pynchon's novel can be seen as a modern repetition and distortion of what is the paradigm novel for Western fiction, *Don Quixote*.

The character called Stencil is the figure (also the copy) who attempts to apprehend and pattern reality according to his single 'ideal' obsession with 'V.' (whatever she – or it – might be). In Lukács's terms, his consciousness is much narrower than the world through which he moves, and everything has to be either 'translated' into terms consonant with his one interpretative scheme or screened out. (His obsession with 'V.' is the clue with which he attempts to find his way through the labyrinth, but in the process he transforms the labyrinth into a useless plethora of clues.) At the other extreme is the figure of Benny Profane, whose consciousness seems to be so wide and unselective that he experiences no *Gestalt* at all in his perceptions of the world around him. For Stencil everything potentially signifies too much, and taken to its logical extreme his mind would conflate the whole of existence into a single sign – 'V'; all differences would finally vanish as the over-integrated world resolved itself into one undifferentiated clue. That it would be a clue to itself indicates the ultimate danger of such a quest, for if V. can mean everything it means nothing. For Benny Profane there are more signals than significances; he detects no clues anywhere and is a motiveless wanderer up and down the generic street of the twentieth century, going nowhere and seeing only separate objects in a disintegrating world. Modern versions and distortions, I suggest, of Don Quixote and Sancho Panza. Is Stencil a lunatic, or a man with some kind of creative vision? Is Benny Profane a pragmatic realist, or a figure of dulled and impoverished perceptions? And between them these two figures point to the question that worries so many of Pynchon's characters. Are we surrounded by plots – social, natural, cosmic; or is there no plot, no hidden configuration of intent, only gratuitous matter and chance?

It is worth noting that this is not a difficult book to read in the way that Joyce's major works, for example, initially are. Each of the fifteen chapters and the Epilogue can be read in what might be called a traditional way. What is confusing initially is the connection between the chapters. Ten chapters are about Benny Profane and the Whole Sick Crew in contemporary America, as often as not involved in chaotic parties or a pointless, destination-less moving around called 'yo-yoing'. Five chapters give accounts from various sources and documents of historical episodes – usually connected with moments of international violence or wars – starting with the Fashoda incident, going on to disturbances in Florence connected with an attempted Venezuelan rebellion and more international plotting and spying, then to a native uprising in German South-West Africa in 1922 which results in a long siege party, then on to an account of the siege of Malta during the Second World War, then back to Paris in 1913 on the brink of the First. The last chapter brings past and present together on Malta at the time of the Suez crisis, while the Epilogue goes back to 1919 when there were riots on the island. The presence of these apparently random episodes from history is largely due to the research work of Stencil.

Stencil and Profane finally travel together to Malta in the last chapter – everything converging on that 'rock' in one way or another – before they finally disappear in their different ways. ('Malta alone drew them a clenched fist around a yo-yo string', p. 437.) Incidents and characters, initially apparently quite unrelated, begin to link up, as possible interconnections begin to emerge. But it is not a matter of piecing together the bits of a jigsaw which is then, as it were, a finished and final picture. Near the end, Stencil's father, a British agent, has the sense that 'Now and again events would fall into ominous patterns' (p. 473); earlier his son Stencil finds a phrase 'cycling round and round' in his head: 'Events seem to be ordered into an ominous logic'. 'He found paper and pencil and began to write the sentence in varying hands and type faces' (p. 443). The relative certainty of the father has declined into an anxious uncertainty in the son – not 'would' but 'seem'. And, in writing out the notion in many different styles and hands, Stencil is doing in little what Pynchon is doing throughout the book, so that the text is marked by a constantly shifting calligraphy, as it were, and we can read it in different ways with differing degrees of certainty and dubiety about whether or not events *are*, or *seem*, 'to be ordered into an ominous logic'. There are many different writings within the book, just as there are many different languages, 'tongues', and group dialects or argots: we should not be too confident about who has the true words – or if there finally are any. Another character, Fausto Maijstral, writes in

43

his confessions about 'learning life's single lesson: that there is more accident to it than a man can ever admit to in a lifetime and stay sane' (p. 317). Is everything 'patterned', ominously or otherwise; or is everything sheer accident? And, according to which 'reading' we incline towards, which way does madness lie? It is just such uncertainties – indeterminacies – that Pynchon's novel generates.

We might consider first Stencil's search for 'V.', which is something of a travesty of the traditional quest for some ultimate truth or goal – or grail. V. is first of all a woman who seems to metamorphose as the century progresses. She appears first as Victoria Wren (Queen Victoria, Christopher Wren?) in Cairo in 1898 and again in Florence in 1899. It is made clear that she was born in 1880. She next appears as Vera Meroving at Foppl's siege party in South-West Africa. This is in 1922, but the chronological jump may be related to the fact that Foppl is trying to re-create the atmosphere in 1904 when von Trotha's troops killed 60,000 natives – a first step towards the great genocides to come. (Meroving may be a slight allusion to the Merovingian dynasty and its endless warfare.) We next read of her 'disassembly' on Malta during the Second World War where she was disguised as 'the Bad Priest'; it is here that she may (though it is not certain) have died. We next read about her in Paris in 1913 where she is known simply as V. and where she has a completely fetishistic lesbian relationship with a young ballerina (it is conducted entirely by mirrors). Her final appearance, in the Epilogue, is in 1919 in Malta as Veronica Manganese where she is rather oddly associated with the Paraclete. I will come back to the nature of her metamorphoses. But 'V' is also a letter, an initial, a sign, a shape which might be seen anywhere – as Stencil bears out. There is the V-Note jazz club; a strange sewer rat named Veronica by a demented priest; a weird fantasy land called Vheissu; Venezuela; Vesuvius; Venus; the Vatican; Queen Victoria; Valletta . . . and so on. So who or what is Stencil searching for? And why?

When Stencil is first mentioned in the book we are given this paragraph of biographical information.

Born in 1901, the year Victoria died, Stencil was in time to be the century's child. Raised motherless. The father, Sidney Stencil, had served the Foreign Office of his country taciturn and competent. No facts on the mother's disappearance.

Died in childbirth, ran off with someone, committed suicide: some way of vanishing painful enough to keep Sidney from ever referring to it in all the correspondence to his son which is available. The father died under unknown circumstances in 1919 while investigating the June Disturbances in Malta. (p. 51)

Just that: abrupt and summary. But it alerts us to the possibility – it can never be more than that – that, whether he knows it or not, Stencil is in search of his mother. In this, too, he would be very much 'the century's child', since one important feature of twentieth-century literature is the loss of a sense of origin. 'Beginnings', as Edward Said calls them, have become increasingly problematical. We can extend this suggestion. If he is the 'century's child', then he is by the same token searching for the century's 'mother' or, more generally, who or what it was that gave birth to the twentieth century and caused it to move so rapidly towards world wars, genocide, nuclear bombs – a whole arsenal of events and inventions, and dehumanizations – which would indeed seem to be accelerating the approach of total entropy. One note in his father's papers (which Stencil memorizes) opens up such a possibility:

There is more behind and inside V. than any of us had suspected. Not who, but what: what is she. God grant that I may never be called upon to write the answer, either here or in any official report. (p. 52)

Stencil is pursuing an unidentifiable 'who' and an indescribable 'what'. But in case we may think of him as some kind of marginal obsessive we must remember that he is indeed 'the century's child'. And there is another aspect to the search. Stencil – and in this he is like Benny Profane – had found that what he most wanted to do was sleep. The impossible search for V. at least provokes him into a kind of activity. But what if the quest succeeded?

Finding her: what then? Only that what love there was to Stencil had become directed entirely inward, towards this acquired sense of animatedness. . . . To sustain it he had to hunt V.; but if he should find her where else would there be to go but back into half consciousness? He tried not to think, therefore, about any end to the search. Approach and avoid.

45

His search for V. must then be asymptotic. 'Life' depends, not on the success, but on the failure of the quest. He is indeed the century's child; for what have so many modern writers and thinkers discovered, if not that what is of vital importance is to be always seeking, never finding?

Stencil is aware that his obsession with 'the letter V' may just be a 'dream', 'a scholarly quest after all, an adventure of the mind': then he will find that it is a 'simple-minded, literal pursuit' (p. 60). We must also read it in both of these ways. But it is notable that he keeps deferring a visit to Malta — because that was where his father died. Again the matter of parental origin both provokes and deflects the search, for it is precisely the father who is responsible for his hopeless quest.

Stencil knows how little he really knows about V. 'She's yielded him only the poor skeleton of a dossier. Most of what he has is inference. He doesn't know who she is, nor what she is. He's trying to find out. As a legacy from his father' (p. 153). She may be a woman, or she may be in some way related to the spirit of history, fitting in 'with the Big One the century's master cabal. . . . If she was a historical fact then she continued active today and at the moment, because the ultimate Plot Which Has No Name was as yet unrealized, though V. might be no more than a sailing vessel or a nation' (p. 225). As the century seems to get more cruel and inhuman, so does V. in her various incarnations. As Victoria Wren she is an admirer of Machiavellian virtu, 'divorced from moral intention' (p. 197). The girl Victoria is 'gradually replaced by V.: something entirely different, for which the young century had as yet no name' (p. 405). As the Bad Priest she advises girls to avoid childbirth and boys to become like rock or crystal. As Father Avalanche glosses this perverse idea: 'seek mineral symmetry, for here is eternal life: the immortality of rock. Plausible. But apostasy' (p. 336). Her own body is increasingly replaced with artificial limbs and bits of inanimate matter. Even when she is 'in love' it is a fetishistic love which is against life: 'so the Kingdom of Death is served by fetish-constructions like V.'s, which represent a kind of infiltration' (p. 406). Stencil even has a daydream of how she would be in the present (1956), 'skin radiant with the bloom of some new plastic; both eyes glass but now containing photoelectric cells, connected by silver electrodes to optic nerves of purest copper wire leading to a brain exquisitely wrought as a diode matrix ever could be' (p. 406) – that is, a complete automaton, a 'triumph' of technology. So the search for V. may be analogous to – identical with – an attempt to trace out the aetiology of twentieth-century history.

But, while Stencil is trying to gather together clues to 'the Ultimate Plot', he is in fact moving further and further into dispersal and uncertainty. Near the end he realizes that 'V. by this time was a remarkably scattered concept' (p. 383), and later recognizes a possible suspicion – 'That it did add up only to the recurrence of an initial and a few dead objects' (p. 438). As the clues 'seem' to come together they also fall apart. Reconstruction is also deconstruction. (While Stencil is assembling his dossier on V., *she* is moving towards her own 'disassembly' on Malta.) What the novel shows is how the 'century's child' may be drawn to a 'cabalistic' imagination, may need some kind of conspiracy theory: it also shows how ambiguous that need might be. This is something that Stencil at least catches a glimpse of: 'Funking out; finding V.; he didn't know which he was most afraid of; V. or sleep. Or whether they were two versions of the same thing' (p. 341). The attempt to establish that everything is part of one big 'plot' might result in a realization that everything is simply 'accident'. We stay awake by vigilantly manœuvring between the two extreme and intolerable possibilities.

I shall return to V., but here it might be appropriate to turn to Benny Profane. If V. is connected to the actual or hallucinated (imagined, projected) world of plot and cabal apocalypse, then Benny is distinctly a creature of the realm of 'accident'. Even 'women had always happened to Profane the schlemihl like accidents: broken shoelaces, dropped dishes, pins in new shirts' (p. 133). He seems to have no motivation, no volition, almost no relationship to the world through which he moves.

> Though the street had claimed a big fraction of Profane's age, it and he remained strangers in every way. Streets had taught him nothing. . . . He walked; walked, he thought sometimes, the aisles of a bright gigantic supermarket, his only function to want. (p. 36)

He drifts through a variety of odd jobs, non-relationships, strange experiences – on the street and under the street – but indeed he learns nothing, not only no skills, but nothing about himself, his world, other people. At the very end, with yet another girl he has met by 'accident', he is saying what he said at the beginning. She says: ' "The experience, the experience. Haven't you learned?" Profane didn't have to think long. "No," he said, "offhand I'd say I haven't learned a goddam thing." ' And while Stencil disappears in pursuit of another totally tenuous clue to V. (a Mme Viola in Stockholm who is said to be an 'oneiromancer and hypnotist' – which may be just what he needs!), Benny Profane appropriately enough vanishes at the end of the street of the twentieth century which for him had never led anywhere. 'Benny and Brenda continued to run through the abruptly absolute night, momentum alone carrying them towards the edge of Malta, and the Mediterranean beyond' (p. 448).

At times there seems to be a vestigial humanity to Benny: he acts – intermittently – as 'guardian' to the girl Paula and once stops her from being raped, and while his relationships with girls all fail he seems – again intermittently – to want to find someone 'for once on the right or real side of the TV screen' (p. 353). Yet he is accused of being 'scared of love' and of being unable 'to give anything' (p. 377), and he does seem more inclined to turn his back and quit than to give and to guard, and more likely to opt for 'the closet' than to try to clear up some of the 'chaos' (to use terms from 'Entropy'). And not only is he physically clumsy and incapable, but he is adrift in language as well: his 'vocabulary it seemed was made up of nothing but wrong words' (p. 135). Not that, with the many 'vocabularies' deployed in the book, we can be sure who, if anyone, has the *right* words. But there is one word that in an odd way relates Benny Profane to V. 'To Profane, alone in the street, it would always seem maybe he was looking for something too to make the fact of his own disassembly plausible as that of any machine' (p. 39). 'Disassembly' – the human turned into the machine: it is what happens to V. And it is notable that when Benny gets tired of one woman talking about love he thinks to himself: 'Someday, please God, there would be an all-electric woman. Maybe her name would be Violet. Any problems with her, you could look it up in the maintenance manual' (p. 379). This, of course, is remarkably like Stencil's fantasy of the V. of the future. Benny Profane might not like a world in which people treat themselves and each other as objects and in various ways replace the animate or human with the inanimate, but he does not or cannot resist it, and it could be said that in effect he is part of it. He is another of the century's children.

The novel opens with a date – 'Christmas Eve, 1955' – and immediately introduces Benny and his 'yo-yo' mode of existence. He is far from being the saviour that the world needs. Who or what might 'save' the world – and how – is one of the central concerns in Pynchon's work, which as well as containing a distinct historical dimension is also permeated (though less visibly) with religious concerns. Problems of 'salvation' can occur at any level – from a drunken party to a planet that seems bent on destroying itself. The problem revealed in the figure of Benny Profane – an inability to communicate, a failure to love, a fading of human feelings into a self-protective indifference – is put into clear focus in an important conversation the jazz musician, McClintic Sphere, has with his girl, Ruby:

'Ruby, what happened after the war? That war, the world flipped. But come '45, and they flopped. Here in Harlem they flopped. Everything got cool – no love, no hate, no worries, no excitement. Every once in a while, though, somebody flips back. Back to where he can love . . .'

'Maybe that's it,' the girl said, after a while. 'Maybe you have to be crazy to love somebody.'

'But you take a whole bunch of people flip at the same time and you've got a war. Now war is not loving, is it?' (p. 291)

This flip/flop problem is in Pynchon's work from the very beginning. As was noted, 'cool' may seem like an appropriate way of surviving in an increasingly inhuman world; but that attitude in itself contributes to inhumanity, or non-humanity, by the denial of love, feeling, concern. That is flop. The switch to flip is, however, ambiguous. To flip is indeed a vernacular word meaning 'to go crazy'. So, as Ruby says, maybe in a cool 'flopped' world you have to go crazy to love, but crazy people do crazy things and a lot of crazy people can be very destructive indeed. 'Make love not war' said a famous slogan of the sixties. The problem is that if you flip you are likely to make love *and* war. There is no saying where a 'flipped' condition might lead you. Is there, then, no other way out of 'flop' than 'flip'? Is there not something in between these two extremes which might not ultimately lead to the same loss of humanity?

McClintic Sphere comes to this conclusion: 'that the only way clear of the cool/crazy flipflop was obviously slow, frustrating and hard work. Love with your mouth shut, help without breaking your ass or publicizing it: keep cool, but care' (p. 360). That last formulation has been criticized as being too easy – slick and glib, like an advertising slogan. But perhaps that is a result of the problem of finding 'right words' in a world in which language seems to be declining like everything else. Keeping cool but caring may not be a prescription for saving the world: it promises no Messianic healing. But it gestures towards some form of maintained humanity in a world in which – in Pynchon's work – an increasing number of people seem to be moving, or have moved, to the extremest states of flop and flip which, as I have said, can seem to end up being the same thing: a very distinct symptom of increased entropy. Both are ways of 'retreating' from humanity; and it is at least *something* to begin to 'retreat from retreat' (p. 313).

Something, but not salvation – certainly not a divine intervention or a restoration of a true sense of 'the sacred'. Having noted a distinctly religious strain in Pynchon's work, I should add that it usually takes the form of yearning or a sense of absence. In this connection I want to note two phenomena in the novel which turn out to be connected – 'tourism' and 'communion'. Literal tourists first appear in the Cairo–Fashoda episode, 'those aged children of Europe, the tourists' (p. 84). In the historical episodes they tend to appear as an increasingly numerous phenomenon. In Florence they prompt Godolphin to some pertinent reflections (Godolphin is the man who penetrated to the fantastic – or fantasy – realm of Vheissu where beneath the dazzling colours of its surface he had a vision of the absolute Nothing which was underneath – and was perhaps at the very centre, or 'heart', of things).

Tourists sauntered by . . . he felt isolated from a human community – even a common humanity. . . . He wondered at this phenomenon of tourism: what was it drove them to Thomas Cook & Son in ever-increasing flocks every year to let themselves in for the Campagna's fevers, the Levant's squalor, the septic foods of Greece. To return to Ludgate

Circus at the desolate end of every season having caressed the skin of each alien place, a peregrine or Don Juan of cities but no more able to talk of any mistress's heart than to cease opening that interminable catalogue. . . . Did he owe it to them, lovers of skins, not to tell about Vheissu, not even to let them suspect the suicidal fact that below the glittering integument of every foreign land there is a hard dead-point of truth and that in all cases – even England – it is the same kind of truth, can be phrased in identical words. (p. 183)

'Lovers of skins' are no lovers at all: 'tourists' of all kinds are perhaps replacing 'human community' and 'tourism' substituting for 'common humanity'. The ideas are drawn together in a remarkable passage near the end of the book. It occurs in the chapter entitled 'V. in love', and she is said to have 'found love at last in her peregrinations through (let us be honest) a world if not created then at least described to its fullest by Karl Baedeker of Leipzig'. (Incidentally, this is one of the two or three occasions when Pynchon uses 'we' or 'us' in the novel; it suggests the presence of an authorial voice which we are bound – or invited – to agree with.) The passage continues:

This is a curious country, populated only by a breed called 'tourists'. Its landscape is one of inanimate monuments and buildings; near-inanimate barmen, taxi-drivers, bellhops, guides. . . . More than this it is two-dimensional as is the Street, as are the pages and maps of those little red handbooks. . . . Tourism thus is supra-national, like the Catholic church, and perhaps the most absolute communion we know on earth: for be its members American, German, Italian, whatever, the Tour Eiffel, Pyramids, and Campanile all evoke identical responses from them; their bible is clearly written and does not admit of private interpretation; they share the same landscapes, suffer the same inconveniences; live by the same pellucid time-scale. They are the Street's own. (p. 404)

The religious parallels only serve to enforce the fact that the 'tourist country' lacks any religious or spiritual dimension (what Henry James called 'the fourth dimension') – not to mention an emotional, human third dimension. And the most important irony is pointed to by the words 'the most absolute communion we know on earth'. 'Communion' looks in one way to notions of community (and communication) and in another, of course, to Holy Communion. It is a word that recurs in varying contexts, some of which I shall cite.

In the Florence episode Evan Godolphin refers to a spreading anxiety:

> the anxiety of everyone living in a world none of us wants to see lit into holocaust. Call it a kind of communion, surviving somehow on a mucked-up planet which God knows none of us like very much. But it is our planet and we live on it anyhow. (p. 192)

Recalling the siege of Malta, Fausto Maijstral describes a condition in which he was 'moving towards that island-wide sense of communion. And at the same time towards the lowest form of consciousness' (p. 311). He adds:

> There is, we are taught, a communion of saints in heaven. So perhaps on earth also in this Purgatory, a communion: not of gods or heroes, merely men expiating sins they are unaware of, caught somehow all at once within the reaches of a sea uncrossable and guarded by instruments of death. (p. 312)

And later: 'Was Fausto believing too much: was the Communion all sham to compensate for some failure as a father and husband?' (p. 327). At one of the endless parties in America, we read of 'one inanimate audio system, fifty jazz enthusiasts and God knows how many bottles of circulating and communal wine' (p. 413). And in the description of the riots on Malta we read: 'mob violence, like tourism, is a kind of communion. By its special magic a large number of lonely souls, however heterogeneous, can share the common property of opposition to what is' (p. 464). Like the 'absolute communion' of tourism, these are all travesties of, or substitutes for (even inversions of), any genuine Holy Communion. The need for some kind of 'communion' seems to be constant, but it can take on degraded forms – anxiety, a siege, a drunken party, mob violence, tourism. There is no contact (communion) with anything transcendental, divine, sacred. In one way or another all the figures are 'tourists' and are 'the Street's own'. They remain profane. Like Benny.

During one of his periods of irregular employment, Benny Profane engages in the hunting down of alligators in the New York sewers (bought as babies for presents, then flushed down into the sewers when people tired of caring for the growing beasts). At one point he has tracked down an alligator, which turns to face him, as though wanting to be shot (only one example of many indications of a spreading death-wish in the world). Benny pauses. 'He waited. He was waiting for something to happen. Something otherworldly, of course. He was sentimental and superstitious. Surely the alligator would receive the gift of tongues' (p. 121). It is a strange moment. The 'gift of tongues' occurred at Pentecost, once alluded to previously in a casual simile in the Fashoda chapter. And it is the only occasion when we are specifically told that Benny was waiting for 'something otherworldly'. It doesn't come for him; arguably it doesn't come for anyone. But the hint is picked up again in a curiously explicit religious passage in the Epilogue. Sidney Stencil (the father) is considering the various possible reactions to 'the prospect of chaos in the streets' (p. 463) threatened by the imminent riots in Malta. Having considered various secular groups, he comes to the church.

> The Church – here perhaps Stencil's C. of E. stuffiness coloured an otherwise objective view – wanted only what the church always desires during times of political crisis. She awaited a Third Kingdom. Violent overthrow is a Christian phenomenon. The matter of a Paraclete's coming, the comforter, the dove; the tongues of flame, the gift of tongues: Pentecost. Third person of the Trinity. None of it was implausible to Stencil. The Father had come and gone. In political terms, the Father was a Prince; the single leader, the dynamic figure whose virtu used to be a determinant of history. This had degenerated to the Son, genius of the liberal love-feast which had produced 1848 and lately the overthrow of the Tsars. What next? What Apocalypse?
>
> Especially on Malta, a matriarchal island. Would the Paraclete be also a mother?
>
> Comforter, true, But what gift of communication could ever come from a woman . . . (p. 465)

At which point his friend, Demivolt, points out a woman sitting at a nearby table – Veronica Manganese. When they

53

meet later they recognize that they have met before, in Florence (when she was Victoria Wren). It is possible (though not, of course, certain) that the father and the 'mother' (of the 'century's child') have converged for a final meeting – which ends with the father's death. (A death associated with the goddess Astarte, the Eastern equivalent to Aphrodite, suggesting perhaps that the sexual drive has been diverted – perverted – into a death-bringing and destructive force in our century.) One critic (W. T. Lhamon, Jr) has interpreted this passage as hinting that V. herself is the Paraclete, or Holy Spirit,[12] but I find this hard to see. Sidney Stencil offers a version of history whereby the Machiavellian stage gave way to a 'liberal' phase which produced revolutions, giving way to – what? Apocalypse? A Second Coming? But we have seen how V. ends as the dismantled, non-human Bad Priest, and we have seen some of the mass atrocities and wars that have marked that third phase. I find no trace that all this will usher in a 'Third Kingdom', unless it be the 'Kingdom of Death'.

In the Epilogue the woman V. is associated with the two kinds of political extremism which were beginning to dominate and determine events in our century – the Right and the Left, emerging and working from apparently opposed places, but ultimately converging in the results they produce. 'The Right can only live and work hermetically, in the hothouse of the past, while outside the Left prosecute their affairs in the streets by manipulated mob violence. And cannot live but in the dreamscape of the future' (p. 461). So Stencil looking at V(eronica) in 1919 perceives this: 'The street and the hothouse; in V. were resolved, by some magic, the two extremes. She frightened him' (p. 480). Right/Left; flip/flop; Stencil/Profane – ultimately they seem to converge and work towards bringing about the same state of affairs. 'Something otherworldly' and a new 'gift of tongues' are hoped for and, by the author, sought for. But it would not do to assume that they have been found. Apocalypse does not *guarantee* Pentecost, and the 'revelations' of an apocalypse may be more horrifying than anything yet seen. Meanwhile we must go on looking for clues among the rubbish and do what we can between 'flipping' and 'flopping', since 'it is our planet and we live on it anyhow'.

One final comment on the status or condition of religion or myth in the world of the book. At one point in contemporary

New York, Benny and some of his American-Italian friends are talking about their work under the street, killing alligators.

> Together on the stoop they hammered together a myth. Because it wasn't born from fear of thunder, dreams, astonishment at how the crops kept dying after harvest and coming up again every spring, or anything else very permanent, only a temporary interest, a spur-of-the-moment tumescence, it was a myth rickety and transient as the bandstands and the sausage-pepper booths of Mulberry Street. (p. 140)

The old myths no longer work: they no longer serve significantly to frame or 'scaffold' the contemporary world (it is worth noting in passing that in chapter 1 we hear of a seaman Ploy, who is transferred from USS *Scaffold* to a mine-sweeper named *Impulsive* – a shift that may be indicative of a desirable change in ways of living in the modern world). In their place we have temporary and transient improvisations using the ephemeral detritus of the modern street. The privileged hierarchies of significance and interpretation of the past must be abandoned, and we must look to the overlooked areas of the contemporary world for new sources of meaning – and perhaps new gifts of tongues. When all the old 'scaffolds' are down, perhaps – *perhaps* – something new and regenerative may appear. Meanwhile, in the fragmenting, self-disassembling, declining world that Pynchon's novel depicts for us, it is clear that no one possesses what Fausto Maijstral wishes for his daughter: 'a single given heart, a whole mind at peace. That is a prayer, if you wish.' It is a prayer that we should all wish to pray.

4

'THE CRYING OF LOT 49'

The Crying of Lot 49 (1966) is one of the most deceptive – as well as one of the most brilliant – short novels to have appeared since the last war. It is a strange book in that the more we learn the more mysterious everything becomes. The more we *think* we know, the less we *know* we know. The model for the story would seem to be the Californian detective story – an established tradition including the works of writers such as Raymond Chandler, Ross MacDonald and Eric Stanley Gardner. But in fact it works in a reverse direction. With a detective story you start with a mystery and move towards a final clarification, all the apparently disparate, suggestive bits of evidence finally being bound together in one illuminating pattern; whereas in Pynchon's novel we move from a state of degree-zero mystery – just the quotidian mixture of an average Californian day – to a condition of increasing mystery and dubiety.

In the simplest terms, the novel concerns Oedipa Maas, who learns that she has been named as an executor ('or she supposed executrix', p. 1) of the estate of a deceased Californian real-estate mogul named Pierce Inverarity. As she sets about exploring this 'estate', she seems to discover more and more clues indicating the existence of an underground, anarchic organization called the Tristero, which, possibly dating from thirteenth-century Europe, seems to oppose all the official lines of communication and have its own secret system of communication. Seems. She can never be sure whether she is discovering a real organization, or is the victim of a gigantic hoax, or is wildly hallucinating. Her search or quest clearly has wider implications, for we are told that Pierce Inverarity was 'a founding father' (p. 14), and near the end we read: 'She had dedicated herself, weeks ago, to making sense of what Inverarity had left behind, never suspecting that the legacy was America' (p. 134).

So on one level the driving question is simply: what does a contemporary American 'inherit' from the country's past? On the title-page Pynchon included this note: 'A portion of this novel was first published in *Esquire* magazine under the title "The World (This one), the Flesh (Mrs Oedipa Maas), and the Testament of Pierce Inverarity".' Since he did not choose to give the title of another extract that appeared in a magazine, we may infer that he wanted this title definitely to appear under the main title of the book. Of course it raises the question: is 'the Testament of Pierce Inverarity' the Devil (following the World and the Flesh)? Like so much in the book it remains a question. The name itself can suggest either un-truth or in-the-truth; I have seen it glossed as 'pierces or peers into variety' and 'inverse' and 'rarity'. But then names can be like that in Pynchon's work, and I shall return to this point in a moment. The last phone call Oedipa receives from Pierce Inverarity is literally multivocal: he speaks in 'heavy Slavic tones', 'comic-Negro', 'hostile Pachuco dialect', as 'a Gestapo officer', and finally 'his Lamont Cranston voice'. He does indeed speak in many 'tongues'; the problem is which, if any of them, is 'true'? The phone call itself comes from 'where she would never know', and the 'phone line could have pointed any direction, any length' (pp. 2–3). Origin, intention, extension – all are insolubly ambiguous. What is Oedipa Maas hearing? What should she listen to? Is it all cacophony? Or is she being somehow singled out for 'revelations'?

I shall consider some details of Oedipa's quest for the meaning of the Pierce Inverarity legacy – and our quest for the meaning of the book (the two being intimately related) – but first I want to quote two crucial passages from the novel. The first occurs shortly after Oedipa has engaged in a sexual game – they call it 'Strip Botticelli' – with the lawyer Metzger. They have been watching a film (in which he starred as a child) in a motel room, and in seeking to anticipate the outcome of the plot (an anticipation of her larger concern to come) she agrees to take off an item of clothing in exchange for every answer he

57

gives to her questions. But she prepares for this by loading herself with endless garments, trinkets and adornments. In doing so she becomes a grotesque image of an insanely eclectic culture which 'over-dresses' itself with bits and pieces of fabrics and fabrications taken from anywhere, and at the same time she reveals a poignant vulnerability, for under the absurd multi-layered 'protection' she is oddly defenceless, naked and exposed. Metzger does not fully undress her but he does seduce her. Later she starts to find clues concerning the Tristero – in a bar, on a latrine wall – and we are given this summarizing paragraph:

> So began, for Oedipa, the languid, sinister blooming of the Tristero. Or rather, her attendance at some unique performance, prolonged as if it were the last of the night, something a little extra for whoever'd stayed this late. As if the breakaway gowns, net bras, jeweled garters and G-strings of historical figuration that would fall away were layered dense as Oedipa's own streetclothes in that game with Metzger in front of the Baby Igor movie; as if a plunge toward dawn indefinite black hours long would indeed be necessary before The Tristero could be revealed in its terrible nakedness. Would its smile, then, be coy, and would it flirt away harmlessly backstage, say good night with a Bourbon Street bow and leave her in peace? Or would it instead, the dance ended, come back down the runway, its luminous stare locked to Oedipa's, smile gone malign and pitiless; bend to her alone among the desolate row of seats and begin to speak words she never wanted to hear? (p. 36)

It is an amazing passage, shifting in tone from vaudeville frivolity to a melodramatic note which is in fact quite chilling. But one important point to note is the conflation of 'performance' with 'historical figuration'. History and theatre become almost interchangeable terms, and Oedipa will never know when she is, or is not, present at some kind of 'performance' – a 'play' which might end in harmless concluding knockabout, or with her hearing 'words she never wanted to hear'. Just what kind of a 'performance' is America putting on anyway? All fun and jollity – or something 'malign and pitiless' coming down the aisles? When – if – history is 'undressed', what will it look like?

Later in the book Oedipa attends an actual theatre to see a performance of a Jacobean play called *The Courier's Tragedy*. Here is a description of a curious change in atmosphere which occurs during the 'performance':

> It is at about this point in the play, in fact, that things really get peculiar, and a gentle chill, an ambiguity, begins to creep in among the words. Heretofore the naming of names has gone on either literally or as metaphor. But now, as the Duke gives his fatal command, a new mode of expression takes over. It can only be called a kind of ritual reluctance. Certain things, it is made clear, will not be spoken aloud; certain events will not be shown onstage; though it is difficult to imagine, given the excesses of the preceding acts, what these things could possibly be. The Duke does not, perhaps may not, enlighten us. Screaming at Vittorio he is explicit enough about who shall *not* pursue Niccolo: his own bodyguards he describes to their faces as vermin, zanies, poltroons. But who then will the pursuers be? Vittorio knows: every flunky in the court, idling around in their Squamuglia livery and exchanging Significant Looks, knows. It is all a big in-joke. The audiences of the time knew. Angelo knows, but does not say. As close as he comes does not illuminate . . . (p. 50)

Those Who Know, know. But what is it they know? What does Oedipa know? And what is the 'big in-joke' anyway? No answers. But notice one thing about this new atmosphere in the play. Before, we are told, 'the naming of names has gone on either literally or as metaphor. But now . . . a new mode of expression takes over. It can only be called a kind of ritual reluctance.' Generally speaking, names can only be used either literally or metaphorically – one of those either/or situations that Pynchon's work is not particularly fond of. Here, then, is a moment, in the story and in the text, when a new mode of expression is inserted between literality and metaphor: an ambiguity, a hesitancy, a 'ritual reluctance'. We, like Oedipa, are teased and drawn into a new and problematical area of semantic dubiety – between the literal and the metaphorical. We – and she – can no longer be sure what 'names' are naming or not naming. Those who 'know' (but what do they know?) do not say. Words come 'close': there are many suggestions – even too many. But no final illumination.

Let us go back to the beginning, and the naming of names. 'Mrs Oedipa Maas' – now what kind of name is that? It is certainly right out of the line of plausibility. Fanny Price, Dorothea Brooke, even Isabel Archer: all well within the realm of possibility. But Oedipa Maas? Not so. So some critics have taken the name as a signal or symbol. Oedipa is a female Oedipus, who was of course the solver of the riddle in one of the first great detective stories in Western literature. But given that the riddle Oedipus finally has to solve concerns his own parents, parricide and incest, and given that this in no way applies to Oedipa, we may pause. Again 'Maas' has been read as suggesting Newton's second law of motion in which 'mass' is the term denoting a quantity of inertia. So the name suggests at once activity and passivity. But this will not do. In Pynchon's texts names do not operate as they do in, for example, Fielding in which Thwackum or Allworthy are – or do – exactly what their names indicate. One critic, Terry Caesar, is probably nearer the mark when he suggests an audible joke in the name: 'Oedipa my ass'; she is no Oedipus at all. As Caesar suggests, noting how wild and improbable – or downright crude and silly – many of Pynchon's 'names' are, he is probably under-mining and mocking the very act of naming. We usually expect to find the person in his or her name. In a realist book as in life, the name comes to signify a real character with unique charac-teristics. This goes along with a very tenacious notion of the unique individual. Pynchon blows all this up. 'Character' and identity are not stable in his fiction, and the wild names he gives his 'characters', which seem either to signify too much (Oedi-pus and Newton indeed!) or too little (like comic-strip figures), are a gesture against the tyranny of naming itself. Lacan sees the fact that we are *named* before we can speak as a symptom of the degree to which we are at the mercy of language itself. Pynchon indicates that he can see how, in various ways, people are subject to the authority of naming: how a whole society can exercise its power through naming. As an author he also has to confer names on his figures, but he does so in such a way as to sabotage the conventional modes of naming. The relationship between individual and name is deliberately problematized – and caricatured – in Pynchon's texts. We find ourselves moving out of the literal or metaphorical and into – well, somewhere else.

We first encounter Oedipa Maas among the eclectic bric-à-brac of contemporary Californian culture, buying lasagne and *Scientific American* in shops that indifferently play Muzak or Vivaldi. When she hears the news about being named as Pierce Inverarity's executrix, she stands in her room 'stared at by the greenish dead eye of the TV tube, spoke the name of God, tried to feel as drunk as possible' (p. 1). Amid the randomness of the thoughts and her surroundings she as it were instinctively turns to the three substitutes for true religion in the contemporary world: the TV (with no message), the name of God (now an empty word) and drink (which doesn't work). So she has to try to start 'sorting it all out', 'shuffling back through a fat deckful of days which seemed . . . more or less identical' (pp. 1, 2). She will have to go on sorting and shuffling to the end — and perhaps beyond.

Then Oedipa's husband 'Mucho' Maas comes back. He had once worked in a used car 'lot' (one of the many linking puns in the book), and Pynchon's elegiac evocation of the sheer pathos of the used car lot is characteristic of his uncanny sensitivity to the suggestive human traces and residues (a kind of information) to be found in the 'used', the rejected, the abandoned refuse and waste of a culture. Mucho now works for a pop music station which sends out an endless stream of jabbering trash (i.e. no information). 'He had believed too much in the lot, he believed not at all in the station' (p. 6). For him every day is a 'defeat': the sadness of the car lot overwhelmed him; the pointlessness of the pop music station empties him out. He can be of no help to Oedipa. Next she receives a middle-of-the-night telephone call from her hysterical psychiatrist (Dr Hilarius), who wants her to join in an LSD experiment he is running. 'But she would be damned if she'd take the capsules he'd given her. Literally damned' (p. 8). No help there. She goes to see her lawyer Roseman, who is mainly concerned with plans to mount a case against the TV lawyer Perry Mason and has no interest in Oedipa and her problem. He merely, vaguely, tries to make crude sexual advances to her. Again, no help. And this sets the pattern of what is to come. All the men who might (should?) help Oedipa recede from her in one way or another — into fantasy, madness, hallucination, some kind of private universe which has no room for any relationships.

The first chapter ends with a reference to her sense of herself

61

as a Rapunzel who, although willing to let her hair down to someone, found that the one time she did so her hair fell out. The man could not reach her: she 'had really never escaped the confinement of that tower' (p. 10). This is followed by her memory of a picture she had seen in Mexico City in which some girls who are imprisoned in a tower are 'embroidering a kind of tapestry which spilled out the slit windows and into a void seeking hopelessly to fill the void' (p. 10). These 'Embroiderers of the Terrestrial Blanket' made Oedipa 'cry'. She cried because she realized that there is 'no escape' for a 'captive maiden'; realized 'that her tower, its height and architecture, are like her ego only incidental: that what really keeps her where she is is magic, anonymous and malignant, visited on her from outside and for no reason at all' (p. 11). As to this conviction concerning the existence of 'anonymous and malignant' magic, the action of the book serves to open up the whole question. For, if it is true, then the only adequate rational reaction would be paranoia. But things are not so simple as that. Before leaving this consideration of what the first chapter opens up, I want to quote one rather strange passage, usually overlooked:

> As things developed, she was to have all manner of revelations. Hardly about Pierce Inverarity, or herself; but about what remained yet had somehow before this stayed away. There had hung the sense of buffering, insulation, she had noticed the absence of intensity, as if watching a movie, just perceptibly out of focus, that the projectionist refused to fix. (p. 10)

'Revelations' is suggestive enough – the word occurs often in the book – and opens up the possibility of a religious dimension to the novel (I'll come back to that). But that sense of something that had somehow remained and yet stayed away, and that absence of intensity which is like a movie slightly out of focus – this suggests strange states of mind, odd intimations of something between presence and absence, a sense of something, an image, a picture, a plot that is not quite visibly *there* but not quite visibly *not* there either. Such strange sensations, which seem to take place at the very interface between meaning and non-meaning, will occur to Oedipa increasingly as she sets out on her quest, alone, to the suitably named city of San Narciso.

As she drives in and looks down at the city ('less an identifiable city than a grouping of concepts', p. 12), she is reminded 'of the first time she'd opened a transistor radio to replace a battery and seen her first printed circuit'.

> Though she knew even less about radios than about Southern California, there were to both outward patterns a hieroglyphic sense of concealed meaning, of an intent to communicate. There'd seemed no limit to what the printed circuit could have told her (if she had tried to find out); so in her first minute of San Narciso, a revelation also trembled just past the threshold of her understanding. (p. 13)

She feels for a moment as though she and her car 'seemed parked at the centre of an odd, religious instant' (p. 13); but a cloud comes, or the smog thickens, and the ' "religious instant", whatever it might've been', is broken up. Again she experiences a kind of brink moment – somewhere between smog and revelation, on the edge or verge of a possible 'religious instant' but the dubiety is, as always, there. There may be a 'concealed meaning . . . an intent to communicate'; but there may not.

'Communicate' (cf. 'communion' in *V.*) is the key word. The novel is concerned with all aspects of communication – voices, postal systems, postage stamps, newspapers, books, radio, TV, telephones, signs on walls, acronyms, drawings, doodlings, etc. Then there is the possibility of some kind of religious communication. Is something being 'revealed' to Oedipa – whether on a sinister secular level, or on a more sacred plane – or is she simply sorting and shuffling clues of very uncertain status and validity? In any case, there are only 'clues', 'never the central truth itself', for if that should blaze out it 'would destroy its own message irretrievably' (p. 69). Communication – if indeed there is any communication – can only be imperfect, incomplete. Oedipa is later to wonder if all the clues that come her way 'were only some kind of compensation. To make up for her having lost the direct, epileptic Word, the cry that might abolish the night' (p. 87). The 'Word' is singular; clues are uncontrollably plural. Having 'lost' – or never having had – the 'Word', Oedipa is doomed to be the recipient/percipient of an ever-increasing number of clues which point to other possible clues which point to other possible clues which . . . there is no end to it. The 'cry' that might have ended the night is replaced by a 'crying' that can only extend it.

To recount Oedipa's encounter with the many possible clues that seem to 'bloom' for her as she pursues her inquiries would be a pointless exercise. From the drawing of a muted horn on a latrine wall to the detailed academic reconstructions and speculations of an English professor (Emory Bortz), the clues and signs seem obvious enough and, regarded in a certain way, seem to cohere. Indeed that becomes part of Oedipa's problem: they are *too* obvious and seem to fit together only too neatly.

> If one object behind her discovery of what she was to label the Tristero System or often only the Tristero (as if it might be something's secret title) were to bring an end to her encapsulation in her tower, then that night's infidelity with Metzger would logically be the starting point for it; logically. That's what would come to haunt her most, perhaps; the way it fitted, logically, together. As if (as she'd guessed that first minute in San Narciso) there were revelations in progress all around her. (p. 28)

As if. Oedipa does indeed become 'sensitized' (starting with the motel seduction) but can hardly be sure just what her new 'sensitized' state is picking up. She may be 'receiving', but who or what is 'sending'?

The state of communication in the everyday world she comes from is zero. When she receives a letter from her husband, she has an intuition that 'the letter would be newless inside' – so she studies the outside for clues instead. When she and Metzger accidentally witness the secret mail distribution of the Peter Pinguid Society at the Scope Bar near the Yoydyne aerospace plant, she discovers that it is indeed an illegal system ('Delivering the mail is a government monopoly', p. 34) which makes use of the Yoydyne inter-office delivery. But, more to the point, the letters delivered have nothing to communicate. The members of this secret society (there are a number of such eccentric societies in the book) simply have a rule that they have to send a letter a week: as Oedipa discovers, they are usually notes with no content. More newless letters. Oedipa's problem is whether she has in fact discovered, stumbled across, been lured by, a *genuinely* alternative mode of communication which does convey real messages in a way that subverts the 'government monopoly' – namely, the Tristero (another name that invites being played with – a meeting with sadness and terror, for example). And, if so, will it release her from her isolation – or confirm it? Will it offer the possibility of real communication 'and revelation' – or like the Peter Pinguid Society system merely reveal a pointless secrecy concealing meaningless, 'newsless' repetitions? If, that is, it exists at all.

The play that Oedipa actually sees – the 'performance' within that larger performance called history – is supposedly by one Richard Wharfinger, a Jacobean dramatist. It is called *The Courier's Tragedy* and is indeed about competing 'communications' systems. It is performed in a theatre located between 'a traffic analysis firm and a wildcat transistor outfit' – that is, between circulation and communication, as Frank Kermode has noted. It concerns another postal monopoly, owned by the Thurn and Taxis family (this seems to be historically accurate); and a rebellious, insurgent counterforce which dedicates itself to subverting, muffling, 'muting' the official system – the Tristero. Oedipa finds herself drawn into 'the landscape of evil Richard Wharfinger had fashioned for his 17th-century audiences, so preapocalyptic, death-wishful, sensually fatigued, unprepared, a little poignantly, for that abyss of civil war that had been waiting, cold and deep, only a few years ahead of them' (p. 44). This, of course, refers to the civil war in England in the seventeenth century. But we should be alert to the fact that any novel about California which refers to '49' is bound to awaken echoes of the Gold Rush of 1849; and at this date too there was a civil war 'waiting' for America 'only a few years ahead' (twelve, in fact). The mining camps in the Gold Rush had their own kind of autonomous, somewhat anarchic organization – well outside any government control – and even, I gather, their own private mail systems. It is also suggested in the book that 1849–50 saw the arrival of the Tristero in America. The novel is making suggestive play with points and echoes in history, just as Wharfinger's macabre play involves the transformation of dead bones into ink, thus seeming to echo or anticipate an episode recounted in the novel in which the bones of dead GI soldiers in the Second World War were brought back from Italy (by the Mafia) and used in cigarette filters or wine. 1849 perhaps – perhaps – offered the possibility of a new kind of America, run and arranged in an entirely different kind of way. But the civil war was just those few years ahead, and the possibility disappeared (or went underground). A century later, 1949, saw the start of the Cold War and the beginning of what was arguably one of America's most conformist periods.

This is all part of the 'performance' of which Oedipa is a witness. In the course of this particular performance of Wharfinger's play there is a shock because it 'names' the 'name' that seemed to have been previously avoided:

> No hallowed skein of stars can ward, I trow,
> Who's once been set his tryst with Trystero.

'Trystero. The word hung in the air as the act ended . . . hung in the dark to puzzle Oedipa Maas, but not yet to exert the power over her it was to' (p. 52). This is Oedipa's crucial 'tryst' with 'Trystero' – the name, the word. It is indeed, chronologically, her first encounter with the actual word; she and the name literally 'meet' just before the middle of the book. And after that she doesn't find clues – the clues find her, indeed, seem to besiege her in every form, while she tries to work out what, if anything, the Tristero really signifies.

The start of chapter 4 (the book has six chapters) makes the change explicit, referring to 'other revelations which now seemed to come crowding in exponentially, as if the more she collected the more would come to her, until everything she saw, smelled, dreamed, remembered, would somehow come to be woven into The Tristero' (p. 58). Her danger – or would it be her deliverance? – is that the 'word' might come to have total 'power over her'. She might then become like Stencil, who 'stencilized' all reality into 'V.'; or she might be moving into a significant discovery about history and the very reality of America itself. Obsession – or revelation. But she tries to go on sorting and shuffling, in the continuing absence of 'the direct, epileptic Word'.

While the word 'Tristero' preoccupies Oedipa, another word equally bothers another of the 'leads' she meets, John Nefastis, and that word – so important in Pynchon – is 'entropy'. As Nefastis explains, 'there were two distinct kinds of this entropy. One having to do with heat-engines, the other to do with communication' (p. 77). Nefastis has a 'machine' based on the Scotch scientist Clerk Maxwell's postulation of something known as Maxwell's Demon. This machine (which Nefastis has tried to make literal) suggests a situation in which there is a box of molecules moving at different speeds and in which 'the Demon' could simply sort out the slow ones from the fast ones: this would create a region of high temperature which could be used to drive a heat engine. 'Since the Demon only sat and sorted, you wouldn't have put any real work into the system. So you would be violating the Second Law of Thermodynamics, getting something for nothing, causing perpetual motion!' To which Oedipa sceptically replies: 'Sorting isn't work?'

The problem here centres on the fact that there seems to be an opposition between thermodynamic entropy and entropy in information theory. As thermodynamic entropy increases in a system, variety and potential diminish, and the certainty of information about the system increases. However, in information theory, 'entropy' refers to the measure of uncertainty in a system. Put very crudely, we can say this: in a thermodynamic system, as things tend towards stagnation, repetition, predictability, they approach a terminal state in which there is no more energy available for new work; in information theory, the higher the degree of disorganization, noise, uncertainty, the more possibility there is for new signals, new information. Nefastis tries to explain:

> She did gather that there were two distinct kinds of this entropy. One having to do with heat engines, the other to do with communication. The equation for one, back in the 30's, had looked very like the equation for the other. It was a coincidence. The two fields were entirely unconnected, except at one point: Maxwell's Demon. As the Demon sat and sorted his molecules into hot and cold, the system was said to lose entropy. But somehow the loss was offset by the information the Demon gained about what molecules were where.
>
> 'Communication is the key,' cried Nefastis. . . . 'Entropy is a figure of speech, then, a Metaphor. It connects the world of thermodynamics to the world of information flow. The Machine uses both. The Demon makes the metaphor not only verbally graceful, but also objectively true.' (p. 77)

His machine has a picture of Clerk Maxwell on it, and if the watcher is a true 'sensitive' he or she will be able to receive and return information from the box, and then the eyes of the portrait will move. But Nefastis is, of course, a lunatic – a 'believer', like so many other figures in the book. A 'believer' not in any genuine faith but in a crazy fantasy of his own making. In the end it emerges that he only wants to have intercourse with Oedipa in front of the television. But it is true that in one form or another 'communication' *is* the key, and Oedipa – demonically or not – will have to go on 'sorting' out the clues (molecules), trying to discover which information really works against entropy as opposed to the kind of non-information ('newsless' letters) that effectively accelerates it. She has to try to decide what kind of revelation or revelations, exactly, she is having.

Some critics regard the novel as unambiguously religious in its implications. What happens to Oedipa, for instance, can be regarded as echoing episodes in the life of Mary, mother of Christ. Then again, after a particularly gruesome scene in *The Courier's Tragedy*, a demented figure named Ercole who has just tortured someone to death (among other things, tearing out his tongue and leaving him to die amid 'tongueless attempts to pray': the possibility of the gift – and the loss – of 'tongues' runs through the book in various forms) says:

> The pitiless unmanning is most meet,
> Thinks Ercole the zany Paraclete
> Descended this malign, Unholy Ghost,
> Let us begin thy frightful Pentecost. (p. 47)

The context perverts the religious words, but perhaps this is a reflection of the perverse Pentecost towards which the book may be moving. As Edward Mendelson has pointed out, 49 is the pentecostal number (the Sunday seven weeks after Easter), but Pentecost derives from the Greek for 'fifty', so the moment at the end of the book when the auctioneer's spread arms are specifically likened to a 'gesture that seemed to belong to the priesthood of some remote culture' (p. 138) is like the moment before a pentecostal revelation when we would all be able to speak in tongues – and understand 'the Word' directly.

The word 'God' is often used, and sometimes seriously. The Tristero system – in its ambiguous aspects – has been seen as representing the sacred dimension to existence, albeit often in a demonic form. Their sign of the muted posthorn may intimate not only a determination to disrupt conventional 'profane' modes of communication but also a determination to block the trumpet of apocalypse. Certainly, although the Tristero may offer some kind of alternative to the apparently 'normal' but utterly alienated irreligious and loveless, and 'narcissistic', life of contemporary society (at least as depicted in the California of the book), their manifestations – if that is what they are – are nearly always sinister and connected with death. Their postage stamps, for instance, distort ordinary stamps by adding something menacing – poisonous flowers, for example, or a head at an impossible angle. On one stamp, which supposedly celebrated 'Columbus Announcing His Discovery' (i.e. of America), 'the faces of three courtiers, receiving the news at the right-hand side of the stamp, had been subtly altered to express uncontrollable fright' (p. 131). So, if we believe everything about the Tristero that seems to come our (or Oedipa's) way, we may conclude that the revelation of a 'sacred' pattern underlying the profane patterns of the surface may be a revelation of ultimate terror and dread. Edward Mendelson has been quick enough to note that the word 'hierophany' which appears in the book (a map Oedipa sees seems to offer 'some promise of hierophany') is not a standard word but a coinage by Mircea Eliade, and he quotes Eliade's definition: 'To designate the *act of* manifestation of the sacred, we have proposed the term hierophany . . . the manifestation of something of a wholly different order, a reality that does not belong to our world, in objects that are an integral part of our natural "profane" world.'[13] This might indeed cover the Tristero very well, though from such a 'sacred' realm that it may well be a very 'unholy ghost' indeed who descends. (Not for nothing are two of the acronyms associated with the Tristero – and with each other – W.A.S.T.E. and D.E.A.T.H.)

On the other hand, seen as a historical phenomenon – an underground movement composed of and standing for 'the Disinherited', which now uses 'silence, impersonation, opposition masquerading as allegiance' (p. 130), and which does have a secret method of communication which allows many 'isolates' (Pynchon deliberately picking up Melville's word, from a context that suggests that all Americans are 'isolates') to 'keep in touch' – the Tristero system would not be the apocalyptic agents of death and doom and God knows what kind of Pentecost, but rather the kind of protoanarchic group with which Pynchon's work shows sympathy. (The founder of the Tristero was 'perhaps a madman, perhaps an honest rebel, according to some a con artist' (p. 199), so, if you want to take the historical account, then the movement was indeed rooted in total ambiguity and dubiety – or plurality of content and intent.)

'Anarchy' is perhaps a crucial clue. During the night when Oedipa lets herself drift through San Francisco she meets an old anarchist acquaintance, Jesus (*sic*) Arrabal. He says to her:

> You know what a miracle is. Not what Bakunin said. But another world's intrusion into this one. Most of the time we coexist peacefully, but when we do touch there's cataclysm. Like the church we hate, anarchists also believe in another world. Where revolutions break out spontaneous and leaderless, and the soul's talent for consensus allows the masses to work together without effort, automatic as the body itself. And yet, sĕná, if any of it should ever really happen that perfectly, I would also have to cry miracle. An anarchist miracle. (pp. 88–9)

The 'anarchist miracle' would not involve the intrusion of the 'sacred' world into our profane one; rather it would be a kind of 'revolution' leading to a whole new way of living together in this world. It would be 'another world' – but still secular. A mundane miracle. Even here the possibility is undermined: Arrabal has an anarchist newspaper with him called *Regeneración*. But the date of the paper is 1904 – a 'communication' so delayed as perhaps to be, literally, out of date.

Oedipa's night of drifting in the Bay Area brings her problems to a head. The whole area is 'saturated' with what seem like clues and references to the Tristero. She even comes across a group of children playing to a song that includes references to 'Tristeroe' and 'taxi' – by which time the clues are becoming worse than meaningless. Her 'sorting' problem has reached its limit. 'Later, possibly, she would have trouble sorting the night into real and dreamed' (p. 86). Possibly. Nothing is certain. As Driblette (the director of *The Courier's Tragedy*) had warned Oedipa: 'You can put together clues, develop a thesis, or several. . . . You could waste your life that way and never touch the truth' (p. 56). It was after seeing that play that Oedipa wrote in her memo book '*Shall I project a world*?' (p. 59). And there is no way in which she can find out how much she is projecting, and how much she is perceiving or receiving. What might be accidental, random, chance, and what might be plotted, determined, purposive, she has no way of establishing; and she gives up trying to 'check out' the possible clues. Her problem is beyond verification or falsification. She has emerged from 'narcissism', but is it only to enter into 'paranoia'? She runs over the possibilities:

> Either you have stumbled indeed . . . onto a secret richness and concealed density of dream; onto a network by which X number of Americans are truly communicating whilst reserving their lies, recitations of routine, arid betrayals of spiritual poverty, for the official government system; maybe even onto a real alternative to the exitlessness, to the absence of surprise to life, that harrows the head of everybody American you know, and you too, sweetie. Or you are hallucinating it. Or a plot has been mounted against you . . . so labyrinthine that it must have meaning beyond just a practical joke. Or you are fantasying some such plot, in which case you are a nut, out of your skull. (p. 128)

Looking at the possibilities, she does not like any of them and just hopes that she is 'mentally ill'. And this is where we feel the full poignancy of her position. 'For this, oh God, was the void. There was nobody who could help her. Nobody in the world' (p. 128).

The problem is finally about America. There is the America of San Narciso, but is there perhaps another America? An America of the 'disinherited' (but 'What was left to inherit?' Oedipa wonders (p. 135)) — transients, squatters, drifters, exiles within the system, people existing in the invisible interstices of official society, like those who live 'among a web of telephone wires, living in the very copper rigging and secular miracle of communication, untroubled by the dumb voltages flickering their miles, the night long, in the thousands of unheard messages' (p. 135). The Tristero system might be a great hoax; but it might be 'all true' (p. 134). And here is perhaps the most crucial and one of the most eloquent and powerful passages in the book:

> Who knew? Perhaps she'd be hounded someday as far as joining Tristero itself, if it existed, in its twilight, its aloofness, its waiting. The waiting above all; if not for another set of possibilities to replace those that had conditioned the land to accept any San Narciso among its most tender flesh without a reflex or a cry, then at least, at the very least, waiting for a symmetry of choices to break down, to go skew. She had heard all about excluded middles; they were bad shit, to be avoided; and how had it ever happened here, with the chances once so good for diversity? For it was now like walking among matrices of a great digital computer, the zeroes and ones twinned above, hanging like balanced mobiles right and left, ahead, thick, maybe endless. Behind the hieroglyphic streets there would be either a transcendent meaning, or only the earth. . . . Ones and zeroes. So did the couples arrange themselves. . . . Another mode of meaning behind the obvious, or none. Either Oedipa in the orbiting ecstasy of a true paranoia, or a real Tristero. For there either was some Tristero beyond the appearance of the legacy America, or there was just America and if there was just America then it seemed the only way she could continue, and manage to be at all relevant to it, was as an alien, unfurrowed, assumed full circle into some paranoia. (pp. 136–7)

The law of the 'excluded middle' – as I understand it – is that a statement is either true or false. There cannot be anything in between. Either it is raining, or it is not. Yet there are those strange, atmospheric conditions, not easily classifiable, in which moistness and dryness seem strangely mixed, which might make us – illogically, unphilosophically – long to admit the 'excluded middle', a middle term for something real but unascertainable. Oedipa is not at ease in a world of binary oppositions – ones and zeroes. Recall that apparently incomprehensible sentence in which it was stated that she would have revelations 'about what remained yet had somehow, before this, stayed away'. The law of the excluded middle would say that either it was there or it was not there. Quite apart from considerations of logic, such a rigidity forecloses on the possibility of unforeseen 'diversity' and irresolvable dubiety. Yet it is into just such an area of possible diversity and dubiety that Oedipa has stumbled – and we, as readers, along with her. Oedipa is mentally in a world of 'if' and 'perhaps', walking through an accredited world of either/or. It is part of her pain, her dilemma and, perhaps, her emancipation. At the auction which concludes the book, leaving all in suspension, the auctioneer is indeed likened to a priest – but also to a 'puppet-master'. There is no way in which Oedipa can be sure just what kind of 'performance' she has been – is – present at. And there is no way in which we can, either. And yet, at the end, as we both finish and wait to begin, something – and this is part of the deceptive magic of the book – seems to remain. Even while it stays away.

5

'GRAVITY'S RAINBOW'

Gravity's Rainbow (1973) is a novel of such vastness and range that it defies – with a determination unusual even in this age of 'difficult' books – any summary. It defies quite a lot of other things as well. There are over 400 characters – we should perhaps say 'names', since the ontological status of the figures that drift and stream across the pages is radically uncertain. There are many discernible, or half-discernible, plots, involving, for example, the GI Tyrone Slothrop, whose sexual encounters in London during the war uncannily anticipate where the V2 rockets fall; a rocket genius named Captain Blicero (later Major Weissmann); Franz Pökler, who worked on the rocket but is hoping to retrieve his wife and daughter from the concentration camps; Tchitcherine, a Soviet intelligence officer (who, among other things, has to impose a Latin alphabet on an illiterate tribe in Central Asia); Enzian, his half-brother and leader of the *Schwarzkommando*, a Herero group exiled in Germany from South-West Africa which is trying to assemble the secrets of the rocket, and which also seems bent on self-annihilation. These plots touch and intersect, or diverge and separate, as the case may be. Somewhere at the back of them all is the discovery by the nineteenth-century German chemist, Kekule von Stradonitz, of the model of the benzene ring, which made possible the manufacture of the molecular structures of plastic and, ultimately, rocketry.

There is a good deal of well-informed technological reference in the book – inserted not gratuitously but to demonstrate how technology has created its own kind of people (servants) with their own kind of consciousness (or lack of it). There is evidence of a whole range of knowledge of contemporary 'specialized' expertises – from mathematics, chemistry and ballistics, to classical music theory, film and comic strips. There is also a prevailing sense of the degree to which modern life has been bureaucratized and turned into an impersonal routine (Max Weber is alluded to and his phrase 'the routinization of charisma' quoted twice – as Edward Mendelson, again, was the first to point out). As before, many other writers are alluded to, directly or indirectly – Melville, Conrad, Faulkner, Emily Dickinson, Whitman, Rilke (crucial), Borges (always important for Pynchon, but in this novel finally named), etc. Out of all this – and much, much more – Pynchon has created a book that is both one of the great historical novels of our time and arguably the most important literary text since *Ulysses*.

I think it is important to stress that the novel provides an exemplary experience in modern reading. The reader does not move comfortably from some ideal 'emptiness' of meaning to a satisfying fullness, but instead becomes involved in a process in which any perception can precipitate a new confusion, and an apparent clarification turn into a prelude to further difficulties. So far from this being an obstacle to appreciating the book, it is part of its essence. It is the way we live now.

Gravity's Rainbow does indeed have a recognizable historical setting. It is engaged with Europe at the end of the Second World War and just after. In choosing to situate his novel at this point in time, Pynchon is concentrating on a crucial moment when a new transpolitical order began to emerge out of the ruins of old orders that could no longer maintain themselves. At one point he describes the movements of displaced people at the end of the war, 'a great frontierless streaming'. The sentences that follow mime out this 'frontierless' condition in an extraordinary flow of objects and people, and conclude: 'so the populations move, across the open meadow, limping, marching, shuffling, carried, hauling along the detritus of an order, a European and bourgeois order they don't yet know is destroyed forever' (p. 551). A later passage suggests what is taking the place of this vanished order. 'Oh, a State begins to take form in the stateless German night, a State that spans oceans and surface politics, sovereign as the International or the Church of Rome, and the Rocket is its soul' (p. 566).

The Rocket is specifically the V2, which was launched on London and, because it travelled faster than sound, crashed before the sound of its flight could be heard – a frightening disruption of conventional sequence and cause–effect expectations. (Hence the famous opening sentence, 'a screaming comes across the sky'.) It also becomes the paradigm product of modern technology, and, in making it the central object of the book, Pynchon is clearly addressing himself to the socio-political implications of contemporary trends in history. But he refuses to do this in a conventional narrative way because conventional narrative procedures were themselves products of that vanished bourgeois order, and it is no longer possible to 'read' what is going on in any conventional manner. Thus Pynchon's characters move in a world of both too many and too few signs, too much data and too little information, too many texts but no reliable editions, an extreme 'over-abundance of signifier', to borrow a phrase from Lévi-Strauss. I stress this first because, before attempting to indicate what the novel is 'about' in any traditional sense, I think it is important to consider how to read it, for more than anything else this book provides an experience in modern reading. People who expect and demand the traditional narrative conventions will be immediately disoriented by this book.

There is one phantasmagoric episode in a 'disquieting structure' which is a dream-version of some contemporary hell. We read: 'It seems to be some very extensive museum, a place of many levels, and new wings that generate like living tissue – though if it all does grow toward some end shape, those who are here inside can't see it' (p. 537). Now not only is this applicable to all the dozens of characters in the book itself – drifting in and out of sections, participating in different spaces, finding themselves on different levels; it is both their *dream* and their *dread* to see an 'end shape' to it all, though of course, being in the book, they never will. But – and I think this is very important – nor do we as readers. One of the things Pynchon manages to do so brilliantly is to make us participate in the beset and bewildered consciousness which is the unavoidable affliction of his characters.

As you read the book you seem to pass through a bewildering variety of genres, behavioural modes, and types of discourse: at different times the text seems to partake of such different things as pantomime, burlesque, cinema, cabaret, card games, songs, comic strips, spy stories, serious history, encyclopedic information, mystical and visionary meditations, the scrambled imagery of dreams, the cold cause-and-effect talk of the behaviourists, and all the various ways in which men try to control and coerce realities both seen and unseen – from magic to measurement, from science to seances. At one point, one character is reading a Plasticman comic; he is approached by a man of encyclopedic erudition, who engages him in a conversation about etymology. Here is a clue for us: we should imagine that we are reading a comic, but it is partly transparent, and through it we are also reading an encyclopedia, a film script, a piece of science history, and so on. There is only one text but it contains a multiplicity of surfaces; modes of discourse are constantly turning into objects of discourse with no one stable discourse holding them together.

This is not such a bizarre undertaking as it may sound. We can all read and decode the different languages and genres Pynchon has brought into his book. Modern man is above all an interpreter of different signs, a reader of differing discourses, a servant of signals, a compelled and often compulsive decipherer. In Henri Lefebvre's use of the word, we do live in a 'pleonastic' society of 'aimless signifiers and disconnected signifieds' on many levels, so that you can see evidence of hyperredundancy in the realm of signs, objects, institutions, even human beings. Wherever we look, there is too much to 'read' ('Is it any wonder the world's gone insane, with information come to be the only real medium of exchange?', p. 258). But never before has there been such uncertainty about the reliability of the texts. One character in the novel, making his way across the wastelands of post-war Europe, wonders whether it does contain a 'Real Text' (p. 520). He thinks that such a text may be connected with the secrets of the rocket; but perhaps the 'Real Text' is the desolate landscape he is traversing, or perhaps he missed the Real Text somewhere behind him in a ruined city . . . Reading Pynchon's novel gives us a renewed sense of how we have to read the modern world. At times in his book it is not always clear whether we are in a bombed-out building or a bombed-out mind, but that too is quite appropriate. For how many of those rockets that fell in London fell in the consciousness of the survivors, exploding in the modern

77

mind? And, looking around and inside us, how can we be sure how much is Real Text, and how much is ruined debris?

In all this it is impossible to say with confidence what the book is 'about', but constantly you have the sense of many things that it seems to be about. We might consider the title, or titles, of the novel. Originally it was to be called *Mindless Pleasures*. We can perhaps infer the intention behind such a title from a passage in which a girl, Jessica, temporarily in love with the rebellious Roger Mexico (of whom more later), thinks of her other suitor, Jeremy, who is the quintessence of the Establishment.

> Jeremy *is* the War, he is every assertion the fucking War has ever made – that we are meant for work and government, for austerity: and these shall take priority over love, dreams, the spirit, the senses and the other second-class trivia that are found among the idle and mindless hours of the day. . . . Damn them, they are wrong. (p. 177)

Pynchon has ever been a sympathetic supporter of 'second-class trivia', which would seem to include those 'mindless' pleasures that have no interest in 'the War', which 'the War' – and all the official organization, technology and bureaucracy it represents (is the product of) – dismisses and disavows. One basic struggle or opposition in the book, then, is indeed between 'mindless pleasures' and the all-too-mindful pains and perversions of 'the War'.

The second title suggests the opposition another way. The 'Rainbow' inevitably triggers reminiscences of the rainbow in Genesis, which was God's covenant to Noah 'and every living creature of all flesh that *is* upon the earth' that there would be no more destruction on the earth. Gravity, by contrast, is that law (not a 'covenant') by which all things – 'and all flesh that *is* upon the earth' – are finally, inexorably, drawn back down and into the earth: an absolutely neutral promise that all living things will die. The trajectory of the rocket – which at the end of the novel is both a womb (it contains the living figure of Gottfried) and a coffin (arguably embodying the death and perversion of all life-giving love and sexuality) – exactly enacts this stark ironic ambiguity. And in this apparently hopelessly proliferating novel the rocket is always there. It is phallic and fatal, Eros transformed into Thanatos, invading 'Gravity's grey eminence' only to succumb to it, curving through the sky like a lethal rainbow, then crashing to the earth. Does it strike by 'chance' or according to some hidden design, some 'music' of annihilation which we shall never hear but which is always being played?

Around the rocket and its production Pynchon builds up a version of wartime England and post-war Europe which is staggering in both its detail and its fantasy. In addition, the novel, as if trying to reach out into wider and more comprehensive contexts, extends back into colonial and American history, down into the world of molecules, up into the stars, back even to Bethlehem when men saw another kind of burning light in the sky. In all this, certain abiding preoccupations may be discerned. Pattern, plots and paranoia – these are familiar in Pynchon's world; add to those paper, plastic, preterition, probability theory and Pavlovian conditioning, and some of the main themes have been listed. (The alliteration is not, of course, accidental: Pynchon, as author, knows that he is engaged in an activity related to Stencil's search for V. Unlike Stencil, however, he is constantly breaking up the gathering pattern of echoes, clues and similarities.)

What emerges from the book is a sense of a force and a system – something, someone, referred to simply as 'the firm' or 'They' – which is actively trying to bring everything to zero and beyond, trying to institute a world of non-being, an operative kingdom of death, covering the organic world with a world of paper and plastic and transforming all natural resources into destructive power and waste: the rocket and the debris around it. 'They' are precisely non-specific, unlocatable. There is always the possibility of a They behind the They, a plot behind the plot; the quest to identify 'Them' sucks the would-be identifier into the possibility of an endless regression. But, whatever Their source and origin, They are dedicated to annihilation. This is a vision of entropy as an extremely powerful worldwide, if not cosmos-wide, enterprise. From Their point of view, and in the world of insidious reversals and inversions They are instituting, the war was a great creative act, not the destruction but the 'reconfiguration' of people and places. They are also identified with 'the System' which removes

79

from the rest of the World these vast quantities of energy to keep its own tiny desperate fraction showing a profit. . . . The System may or may not understand that it's only buying time . . . [that it] sooner or later must crash to its death, when its addiction to energy has become more than the rest of the World can supply. . . . Living inside the System is like riding across the country in a bus driven by a maniac bent on suicide. (p. 412)

The ecological relevance of this is all too frighteningly obvious.

Inside the System everything is fixed and patterned, but its organizing centre – its 'soul' – is the rocket. To the extent that the System and everyone inside the System in one way or another converge on the rocket, they are converging on death. Outside the System, and one of its by-products as it were, is the Zone in which nothing is fixed and there are no patterns or points of convergence. There are 'no zones but the Zone' (p. 333) says one voice. This is the area of 'the new Uncertainty': 'in the Zone categories have been blurred badly' (p. 303). In the Zone everything and everyone is adrift, for there are no taxonomies, and no narratives, to arrange them. If all the concepts are blurred, can the people in the Zone have any knowledge of reality, or are they perhaps nearer to reality by living in a deconceptualized state, fumbling around among the debris left when the prisonhouse of language itself seems to have been destroyed? In the Zone there are only 'images of Uncertainty'. This involves a release from feeling that one is living in a completely patterned and determinate world, but also a panic at being outside any containing and explaining 'frame' (in his review Richard Poirier wrote at length on the significance of the 'frame' throughout the book). Those outside the System seem doomed to go on 'kicking endlessly among the plastic trivia, finding in each Deeper Significance, and trying to string them all together . . . to bring them together, in their slick persistence and our preterition . . . to make sense out of, to find the meanest sharp sliver of truth in so much replication, so much waste' (p. 590).

Figures in the book inhabit either the System or the Zone or move between them (or do not know whether they are in either or both, for of course System and Zone have no locational as well as no epistemological stability), and this in turn elicits two dominant states of mind: paranoia and anti-paranoia. Paranoia is, in terms of the book, 'nothing less than the onset, the leading edge, of the discovery that *everything is connected*, everything in the Creation, a secondary illumination – not yet blindingly One, but at least connected' (p. 703). Of course, everything depends on the nature of the connection, the intention revealed in the pattern; and just *what* it is that may connect everything in Pynchon's world is what worries his main characters, like Slothrop. Paranoia is also related to the Puritan obsession with seeing signs in everything, particularly signs of an angry God. Pynchon makes the connection clear by referring to 'a Puritan reflex of seeking other orders behind the visible, also known as paranoia' (p. 188). The opposite state of mind is anti-paranoia, 'where nothing is connected to anything, a condition not many of us can bear for long' (p. 434). (This may be a reference to the lines in *The Waste Land*:

> On Margate Sands.
> I can connect
> Nothing with nothing. ('The Fire Sermon'))

And, as figures move between System and Zone, so they oscillate between paranoia and anti-paranoia, shifting from a seething blank of unmeaning to the sinister apparent legibility of an unconsoling labyrinthine pattern or plot. 'We are obsessed with building labyrinths, where before there was open plain and sky. To draw ever more complex patterns on the blank sheet. We cannot abide that *openness*; it is terror to us' (p. 264). Those who do not accept the officially sanctioned 'delusions' of the System as 'truth', but cannot abide pure blankness, have to seek out other modes of interpretation. Thus 'Those like Slothrop, with the greatest interest in discovering the truth, were thrown back on dreams, psychic flashes, omens, cryptographies, drug-epistemologies, all dancing on a ground of terror, contradiction, absurdity' (p. 582). This is the carnival of modern consciousness which the book itself portrays.

All this is related to our situation as readers. To put it very crudely, the book dramatizes two related assemblings and disassemblings – of the rocket, and of the character or figure named Slothrop. Slothrop is engaged in trying to find out the secret of how the rocket is assembled, but in the process he himself is disassembled. Similarly the book both assembles and disassembles itself as we try to read it. For, just as many of the characters are trying to see whether there is a 'text' within the 'waste' and a 'game behind the game' (p. 208), that is what we are having to do with the book as it unfolds in our attention. There is deliberately too much evidence, partaking of too many orders of types of explanation and modes of experience for us to hold it all together. Reading itself thus becomes a paranoid activity which is, however, constantly breaking down under the feeling that we shall never arrive at a unitary reading, never hold the book in one 'frame': the sense of indeterminateness is constantly encroaching on us. We fluctuate between System and Zone, paranoia and anti-paranoia, experiencing both the dread of reducing everything to one fixed explanation – an all-embracing plot of death – and the danger of succumbing to apparently random detritus.

Behind all this is the process of nature itself, working by organization and disorganization. The rocket is described as 'an entire system *won*, away from the feminine darkness, held against the entropies of lovable but scatterbrained Mother Nature' (p. 324). It engorges energy and information in its 'fearful assembly'; thus its 'order' is obtained at the cost of an increase in disorder in the world around it, through which so many of the characters stumble. But in its fixity and metallic destructive inhumanity it is an order of death – a *negative* parallel of the process of nature, since its disintegration presages no consequent renewal and growth. That is one reason why at the end the rocket is envisaged as *containing* the living body of a young man (Gottfried), for this is the System *inside* which man is plotting his own annihilation. If we as readers try to win away one narrative 'system' from the book, we are in danger of repeating mentally what They are doing in building the rocket. To put it in its most extreme form, They are trying to reduce all of nature's self-renewing variety to one terminal rocket; we must avoid the temptation to reduce the book to one fixed meaning. That is why our reading should be paranoid and anti-paranoid, registering narrative order and disorder, experiencing both the determinate and the indeterminate,[14] pattern and randomness, renewing our awareness of our acts and interpretations as being both conditioned and free, and of ourselves as synthesizing and disintegrating systems.

In this way we can to some extent be released from the System—Zone bind which besets Pynchon's main characters, in particular the figure of Slothrop. What happens to Slothrop is in every sense exemplary. One of the earliest events in his life is being experimented on in a Pavlovian laboratory (which is related to the obsession with all kinds of control and 'conditioning' that the book also explores). He is last seen, if seen at all, on a record cover. In between he has been the Plasticman and Rocketman of the comics he reads, played a variety of roles for English and American intelligence, been involved in the distorted fantasies and plots of dozens of figures in post-war Europe, all the time approaching the centre, the secret of the rocket, which is also the absolute zero at the heart of the System. He knows that he is involved in the evil games of other people, whether they are run by the army or black-marketeers or whatever, but he cannot finally get out of these games. Indeed, leaving all the games is one of the hopes and dreams of the few people with any human feeling left in the book. But it remains a dream. (This is problematical. Of one character we read: 'Pökler committed then his act of courage. He quit the game' (p. 430). And an earlier comment seems to allow of this possibility:

> But now and then, players in a game will, lull or crisis, be reminded how it is, after all, really play – and be unable then to continue in the same spirit. . . . Nor need it be anything sudden, spectacular – it may come in gentle – and regardless of the score, the number of watchers, their collective wish, penalties they or the Leagues may impose, the player will, waking deliberately . . . say *fuck it* and quit the game, quit it cold . . . (p. 107)

The problem is that there seems to be nowhere to go if you 'quit the game' – though I suppose it could be an internal secession – unless it means to get lost in the Zone. But that is not an unequivocal experience.)

Reality has been pre-empted by games, or it has been replaced by films, so that people can be said to live 'paracinematic lives'. As Slothrop moves through different experience-spaces, he suffers a loss of emotion, a 'numbness', and a growing sense that he will never 'get back'. Along with this erosion of the capacity to feel, he begins to 'scatter', his 'sense of Now' or 'temporal bandwidth' gets narrower and narrower, and there is a feeling that he is getting so lost and unconnected that he is vaporizing out of time and place altogether. Near the end of his travels, Slothrop suddenly sees a rainbow, a real one, and he has a vision of its entering into sexual union with the green unpapered earth; it is the life-giving anithesis to the rocket's annihilating penetrations: 'and he stands crying, not a thing in his head, just feeling natural' (p. 626). After that he effectively vanishes. There is a story told about him.

> [He] was sent into the Zone to be present at his own assembly – perhaps, heavily paranoid voices have whispered, *his time's assembly* – and there ought to be a punch line to it, but there isn't. The plan went wrong. He is being broken down instead, and scattered. (p. 738)

The disassembling of Slothrop is, as I have suggested, in some way related to the assembling of the rocket – the plan that went *right* – and it has far-reaching and disturbing implications.

The last comment on the possible whereabouts of Slothrop is this: 'we would expect to look among the Humility, among the gray and preterite souls, to look for him adrift in the hostile light of the sky, the darkness of the sea' (p. 742). This idea of 'the preterite' is very important in this book and, I think, central to Pynchon's vision; as he uses it, it refers to those who have been 'passed over', those he has always been interested in, the abandoned, the neglected, the despised and the rejected, those for whom the System has no use, the human junk thrown overboard from the ship of state (a literal ship in this book, incidentally, named *Anubis* after the ancient Egyptian God of the Dead). Set against the preterite are the élite, the users and manipulators, those who regard the planet as solely for their satisfaction, the nameless and ubiquitous 'They' who dominate the world of the book. One of the modern malaises Pynchon has diagnosed is that it is possible for a person to feel himself entering into a state of 'preterition'. But – and once again Pynchon's erudition and wit work admirably here – the idea of humanity being divided into a preterite and an élite or elect is of course a basic Puritan belief. In theological terms, the preterite were precisely those who were not elected by God and, if I may quote from one of those chilling Puritan pronouncements, 'the preterite are damned because they were never meant to be saved'. In redeploying these terms, which after all were central to the thinking of the people who founded America, and applying them to cruelly divisive and oppositional modes of thought at work throughout the world today, Pynchon once again shows how imaginatively he can bring the past and present together.

One of Slothrop's ancestors wrote a book called *On Preterition*, supporting the preterite as being quite as important as the elect, and Slothrop himself wonders whether this doesn't point to a fork in the road which America never took, and whether there might not be a 'way back' even in the ruined spaces of post-war Europe:

> maybe for a little while all the fences are down, one road as good as another, the whole space of the Zone cleared, depolarized, and somewhere inside the waste of it a single set of coordinates from which to proceed, without elect, without preterite, without even nationality to fuck it up . . .
> (p. 556)

This, then, is the organizing question of the book. Is there a way back? (Page 1 signals this question: 'Is this the way out?') Out of the streets 'now indifferently gray with commerce'; out of the City of Pain, which Pynchon has taken over from Rilke's Tenth Duino Elegy and offers as a reflection of the world we have made; a way back out of the cinemas, the laboratories, the asylums and all our architecture of mental drugging, coercion and disarray (derangement)? Out of a world in which emotions have been transferred from people to things, and where images supplant realities? Where, ultimately, would the 'way back' lead, if not to some lost Eden previous to all categories and taxonomies, election and preterition, divisions and oppositions? Can we even struggle to regain such a mythic state? Of course the book offers no answers, though the possibility of a 'counterforce' is touched on.

The last section of the novel is indeed entitled 'The Counterforce', and one figure, Tchitcherine, is convinced 'There is a counterforce in the Zone' (p. 611). But if there is an active 'counterforce' it would seem to be vitiated by its contact with, and contamination by, the System. A crucial figure in this possible counterforce is Roger Mexico, and here are some of his late doubts about its viability or possible effectiveness.

85

Well, if the Counterforce knew better what those categories concealed, they might be in a better position to disarm, de-penis and dismantle the Man. But they don't. Actually they do, but they don't admit it. Sad but true. They are as schizoid, as double-minded in the massive presence of money, as any of the rest of us, and that's the hard fact. The Man has a branch office in each of our brains, his corporate emblem is a white albatross, each local rep has a cover known as the Ego, and their mission in this world is Bad Shit. We do know what's going on, and we let it go on . . . which is worse: living on as Their pet, or death? It is not a question he has ever imagined himself asking seriously. It has come by surprise, but there's no sending it away now, he really does have to decide, and soon enough, plausibly soon, to feel the terror in his bowels. Terror he cannot think away. He has to choose between his life and his death. Letting it sit for a while is no compromise, but a decision to live, on Their terms . . . (pp. 712–13)

In the event, all that Roger Mexico achieves (along with Seaman Bodine, an old Pynchon figure) is the disruption of an official dinner with obscene language. It is a gesture against the binding power of the official language, but not much more.

We hear no more of Roger Mexico after this incident. But, in a world dominated by the firm, the System, They, he does represent two crucial potential 'counterforces' – in brief, 'probability' and love. There are a number of references to probability theory in the book, and their relevance can be appreciated if we recall Oedipa Maas caught between zeroes and ones as she found herself forced into a mental prison of binary oppositions at the end of *Lot 49*. In *Gravity's Rainbow* the behaviourist Pavlovian scientist Pointsman is absolutely a zero/one man, and 'If ever the Antipointsman existed, Roger Mexico is the man' (p. 55) – because Mexico, who works with 'probability', can exist and operate in those 'excluded middles' that in Pynchon represent the area of unforeseen possibilities and diversities. One passage makes this clear:

But in the domain of zero to one, not-something to something, Pointsman can only possess the zero and the one. He cannot, like Mexico, survive anyplace in between. . . . But to Mexico belongs the domain *between* zero and one – the middle Pointsman has excluded from his persuasion – the probabilities (p. 55)

It has the effect of keeping open a gap in the systematized and systematic thinking of the System. That thinking can only accept cause-and-effect thinking, because that makes possible a fantasy of total control ('*We must never lose control*', thinks Pointsman, p. 144); but Mexico can see further:

> there's a feeling about that cause-and-effect may have been taken as far as it will go. That for science to carry on at all, it must look for a less narrow, a less . . . sterile set of assumptions. The next great breakthrough may come when we have the courage to junk cause-and-effect entirely, and strike off at some other angle. (p. 89)

Striking off at 'some other angle' would involve recognizing and accepting 'probability', 'indeterminacy' and 'discontinuity' in the 'curve of life' (p. 664). All these modes of thought are enacted in the text itself (we are seldom confronted with zero/one choices; more often we find ourselves groping away in the forgotten richness – and darkness – of those excluded middles). But whether they are sufficient to *act* as a counterforce is less clear.

It might be asked if there are any other hints of effective positives – counterforces – in the book. Roger Mexico is one of the very, very few figures who experience a genuine kind of 'love' (with Jessica), based on real feeling, mutuality, loss of ego, true sensuality. But their love episode is, as it were, a furtive piece of borrowed time during the war; it does not survive, and Jessica turns to the Establishment figure of Jeremy as 'safer'. There is indeed very little love in the book: perversion and betrayal (the children especially suffer) seem to dominate, not to mention various forms and degrees of extermination and mutilation. Religious hope is teasingly glimpsed at. During the truly astonishing passage describing the Christmas vespers attended by Roger and Jessica, with reference to the magi Pynchon writes:

> Will the child gaze up from his ground of golden straw then, gaze into the eyes of the old king who bends long and unfurling overhead, leans to proffer his gift, will the eyes meet, and what message, what possible greeting or entente

will flow between the king and the infant prince? Is the baby smiling, or is it just gas? Which do you want it to be? (p. 131)

The text suddenly flashes a half-ironic choice at us – to leave us unsettled between miracle and technology. But it hardly suggests any coming kind of salvation or true transcendence. Indeed, most of the figures in the book are somewhat like Barnardine in *Measure for Measure* (to turn again to what is obviously an important play for Pynchon), 'insensible of mortality, and desperately mortal' (IV. ii). After the Advent service Roger and Jessica long for

> another night that could actually, with love and cockcrows, light the path home, banish the Adversary, destroy the boundaries between our lands, our bodies, our stories, all false, about who we are: for the one night, leaving only the clear way home and the memory of the infant you saw. (p. 135).

But they find no such 'clear way home' and have to look for 'the path you must create by yourself, alone in the dark' (p. 136). And that is the situation of most of the figures in the book. There are some traces of decent human feeling: strangers occasionally help, and among the 'Humility' there are still 'a few small chances for mercy' (p. 610). Kindness is mentioned – 'kindness is a sturdy enough ship for these oceans' (p. 21) – but is insufficiently practised. Positive, generous, good human feelings and hopes and aspirations have not entirely vanished, but they are everywhere in retreat, and the attrition rate among them is dire. The counterforce (or counterforces) may have some kind of vestigial or underground existence. But it is not to be counted on.

There are recurring dreams of 'freedom' – never realized – but if there is any hope it seems to reside in 'the Earth': Enzian dreams that 'Somewhere, among the wastes of the World, is the key that will bring us back, restore us to our Earth and to our freedom' (p. 525), and in a late section headed 'Streets' that hope is again inscribed: 'But in each of these streets, some vestige of humanity, of Earth, has to remain. No matter what has been done to it, no matter what it's been used for' (p. 693).

This perhaps desperate faith in the regenerative powers of 'the Earth' accounts, I think, for a rather strange episode which follows immediately after the opening scene of the book. Pirate Prentice (the first named figure in the book, and of distinct importance) holds one of his Banana Breakfasts. Up on the roof of his maisonette in London there is a heap of old earth (and dead leaves and vomit and other decaying bits of organic life) – 'all got scumbled together, eventually, by the knives of the seasons, to an impasto, feet thick, of unbelievable black topsoil in which anything could grow, not the least being bananas' (p. 5). So, in the midst of the destruction of war, growth, willy-nilly, continues. The Banana Breakfast is a fairly chaotic, farcical affair, but the bananas themselves – an unlikely enough presence in wartime London – signal a crucial phenomenon.

> Now there grows among all the rooms . . . the fragile, musaceous odor of Breakfast: flowery, permeating, surprising, more than the color of winter sunlight, taking over not so much through any brute pungency or volume as by the high intricacy to the weaving of its molecules, sharing the conjuror's secret by which – though it is not often Death is told so clearly to fuck off – the living genetic chains prove even labyrinthine enough to preserve some human face down ten or twenty generations . . . so the same assertion-through-structure allows this war morning's banana fragrance to meander, repossess, prevail. Is there any reason not to open every window, and let the kind scent blanket all Chelsea? As a spell, against falling objects . . . (p. 10)

The banana – a comic enough 'spell' to set against the rocket – is nevertheless evidence of that endless generative power of the earth, that 'assertion-through-structure' which is the one real hope – perhaps the only genuine counterforce – against 'Their several entropies' (p. 302), and that accelerating movement towards death which seems to mark so many areas of the book.

The book moves to a climax that is a sort of terminal fusion of many of the key fantasies and obsessions in the book. It takes place in the American West ('of course Empire took its way westward, what other way was there but into those virgin sunsets to penetrate and to foul?'; Pynchon's book follows), and it should be noted that the last section as a whole becomes extremely difficult – impossible – to 'follow' in any way at all, as though the book demonstrates how any kind of narrative that seems to link together fragments and images is becoming impossible. The warning has been sounded earlier on: 'Nobody ever said a day has to be juggled into any kind of sense at day's end' (p. 204) – or a book at book's end. Indeed, we are systematically juggled out of sense (any recognizable sense, at least), not allowed that repose and reassurance that any sense of completed narrative can bring. Yet the very last moment seems clear enough – and sufficiently disturbing. The opening page of the novel evokes the evacuation of London, with a crucial interposed comment: 'but it's all theatre'. On the very last page we are back in a theatre. We are waiting for the show to start; as Pynchon comments, we have 'always been at the movies (haven't we?)'. The film has broken down, though on the darkening screen there is something else – 'a film we have not learned to see'. The audience is invited to sing, while outside the rocket 'reaches its last unmeasurable gap above the roof of this old theatre'. It is falling in absolute silence, and we know that it will demolish the old theatre – the old theatre of what is left of our civilization. But we don't see it because we are *in* the theatre trying to read the film behind the film; and we won't hear it because, under the new dispensation, the annihilation arrives first, and only after 'a screaming comes across the sky'.

To argue on behalf of Pynchon's importance as a writer would be supererogatory. Placing him in a larger context is more difficult. More difficult, because he seems aware of all the literature that preceded him as well as the writing that surrounds him. From one point of view, he emerges from that extraordinary proliferation of experimentation in the novel which so deeply shaped the direction of American fiction during the 1960s and 1970s. Thus he takes his place in a period of American writing that includes such authors as William Burroughs, Joseph Heller, John Hawkes, John Barth, Robert Coover, Rudolph Wurlitzer, Ishmael Reed, Norman Mailer, Saul Bellow, and many others. The aesthetic funds alive at this time were various, but in particular I believe he was affected by the work of William Gaddis, whose novel *The Recognitions* (1955) exerted a general influence that has yet to be fully traced. This generation of American writers was in turn influenced by many European and South-American writers – in particular, Jorge Luis Borges and Vladimir Nabokov, but also Samuel Beckett, Italo Calvino, Gabriel Garcia Marquez, Alain Robbe-Grillet and Günter Grass. That list could be extended; but suffice it to say that Pynchon was writing his novels during an extraordinarily rich time of ferment and innovation in the contemporary novel, and quickly became one of its essential voices.

However, looked at from another angle, Pynchon's work takes its place in that line of dazzlingly daring, even idiosyncratic American writing which leads back through writers like Faulkner to Mark Twain and Hawthorne, and above all to Melville and *Moby-Dick*. And, taking yet another view, we might want to cite *Tristram Shandy* as an earlier experimental novel that lies behind him; but then Sterne points us in turn back to Rabelais, and both bear the mark of *Don Quixote* (as does Pynchon) — which is, in a manner of speaking, where the novel as we know it in the West began. Few major modern writers have not in some fashion returned to these origins, and thus we can see Pynchon continuing that series of radical shifts and innovations in fictional technique which was started by Conrad and James, and continued by Joyce — all of whom are more or less audible in his work. Which is all to say that he is both creatively eclectic and unmistakably original. From one point of view, the novel from its inception has always been a mixed genre with no certain limits or prescribed formal constraints; Pynchon, then, is in no way an 'eccentric' novelist, for the novel has no determined centre. Rather he is a key contemporary figure in the great tradition of those who extend the possibilities of fiction-making in arresting and enriching ways — not in this or that 'Great Tradition', but in the great tradition of the novel itself.

NOTES

1 Roland Barthes, 'The Death of the Author', in *Image-Music-Text*, essays selected and translated by Stephen Heath (London: Fontana, 1977), pp. 142–9.

2 J. Fenimore Cooper, *The American Democrat* (New York: Vintage Books, 1956), p. 129.

3 *Letters of Emily Dickinson* (Cambridge, Mass.: Harvard University Press and Belknap Press, 1958), p. 972.

4 Matthew Winston, 'The Quest for Pynchon', in George Levine and David Leverenz (eds), *Mindful Pleasures: Essays on Thomas Pynchon* (Boston, Mass.: Little, Brown, 1976), Appendix.

5 Michael Thompson, *Rubbish Theory* (London: Oxford University Press, 1979), p. 2.

6 Ibid., p. 9.

7 Ibid., p. 11.

8 Ibid., p. 88.

9 Edgar Allan Poe, 'A Few Words on Secret Writing', *Graham's Magazine* (July 1841).

10 Georg Lukács, *The Theory of the Novel* (London: Merlin Press, 1971), p. 97.

11 Ibid., pp. 103–4.

12 W. T. Lhamon, Jr, 'Pentecost, Promiscuity, and Pynchon's *V*.', in Levine and Leverenz (eds), op. cit.

13 Mircea Eliade, *The Sacred and the Profane* (New York: Harcourt Brace, 1959), p. 11.

14 I was sent a very interesting essay on 'indeterminacy' in *Gravity's Rainbow* by Melvin Ulm and David Holt at Ohio State University, in which they suggest the relevance of the work of W. V. Quine – in particular, *Word and Object* – in considering what Pynchon is doing in the novel. To my knowledge the essay has not been published, but it does contain some fruitful ideas which merit attention, and I wish to acknowledge that I profited from reading it.

BIBLIOGRAPHY

WORKS BY THOMAS PYNCHON

Short fiction

'The Small Rain'. *The Cornell Writer*, 6 (March 1959).
'Mortality and Mercy in Vienna'. *Epoch*, 9 (Spring 1959).
'Low Lands'. *New World Writing*, 16 (1960).
'Entropy'. *Kenyon Review*, 22 (1960).
'Under the Rose'. *Noble Savage*, 3 (1961).
'The Secret Integration'. *Saturday Evening Post*, 237 (19 December 1964).
'The World (This One), The Flesh (Mrs Oedipa Maas), and The Testament of Pierce Inverarity'. *Esquire*, 64 (December 1965).
'The Shrink Flips'. *Cavalier*, 16 (March 1966).

Article

'A Journey into the Mind of Watts'. *New York Times Magazine*, 12 June 1966.

Novels

V. Philadelphia, Pa: Lippincott, 1963. London: Cape, 1963.
The Crying of Lot 49. Philadelphia, Pa: Lippincott, 1966. London: Cape, 1967.
Gravity's Rainbow. New York: Viking Press, 1973. London: Cape, 1974.

BIBLIOGRAPHY

Herzberg, Bruce. 'Selected Articles on Thomas Pynchon: An Annotated Bibliography'. *Twentieth Century Literature*, 21, 2 (May 1975).

Weixlmann, Joseph. 'Thomas Pynchon: A Bibliography', *Critique*, 14, 2 (1972).

For more recent bibliographical information, see *Pynchon Notes*, ed. John M. Krafft and Khachig Tölölyan, obtainable from Khachig Tölölyan, English Department, Wesleyan University, Middletown, CT 16457, USA. Six issues have appeared to date.

SELECTED CRITICISM OF THOMAS PYNCHON

Books

Cowart, David. *Thomas Pynchon: The Art of Allusion*. Carbondale, Ill.: Southern Illinois University Press, 1980.

Levine, George, and Leverenz, David (eds). *Mindful Pleasures: Essays on Thomas Pynchon*. Boston, Mass.: Little, Brown, 1976.

Mendelson, Edward (ed.). *Pynchon: A Collection of Critical Essays*. Englewood Cliffs, NJ: Prentice-Hall, 1978.

Pearce, Richard (ed.). *Critical Articles on Thomas Pynchon*. Boston, Mass.: G. K. Hall, 1981.

Pétillon, Pierre-Yves. *Le Grand'route: espace et écriture en Amérique*. Paris: Seuil, 1979.

Plater, William. *The Grim Phoenix*. Bloomington, Ind.: Indiana University Press, 1978.

Siegel, Mark. *Creative Paranoia in Gravity's Rainbow*. Port Washington, NY: Kennikat Press, 1978.

Slade, Joseph. *Thomas Pynchon*. New York: Warner Paperbacks, 1974.

Selected articles

Abernathy, Peter L. 'Entropy in Pynchon's *The Crying of Lot 49*'. *Critique*, 14, 2 (1972).

Davis, Robert M. 'Parody, Paranoia, and the Dead End of Language in *The Crying of Lot 49*'. *Genre*, 5 (1972).

Friedman, Alan J., and Puetz, Manfred. 'Science and Metaphor: Thomas Pynchon and *Gravity's Rainbow*'. *Contemporary Literature*, 15 (Summer 1974).

Golden, Robert E. 'Mass Man and Modernism: Violence in Pynchon's *V.*'. *Critique*, 14, 2 (1972).

Kermode, Frank. 'The Use of the Codes'. In Seymour Chatman (ed.), *Approaches to Poetics*. New York: Columbia University Press, 1973.

Kodony, Anette, and Peters, Daniel J. 'Pynchon's *The Crying of Lot 49*'. *Modern Fiction Studies*, 19 (Spring 1973).

Ozier, Lance W. 'Antipointsman/Antimexico: Some Mathematical Imagery in *Gravity's Rainbow*'. *Critique*, 16, 2 (1974).

——'The Calculus of Transformation: More Mathematical Imagery in *Gravity's Rainbow*'. *Twentieth Century Literature*, 21, 2 (May 1975).

Patteson, Richard. 'What Stencil Knew: Structure and Certitude in Pynchon's *V.*'. *Critique*, 16, 2 (1974).

Redfield, Robert, and Hays, Peter. 'Fugue as Structure in Pynchon's "Entropy" '. *Pacific Coast Philology*, 12 (1977).

Richter, D. H. 'The Failure of Completeness: Pynchon's *V.*'. In *Fable's End: Completeness and Closure in Rhetorical Fiction*. Chicago, Ill.: University of Chicago Press, 1975.

Sanders, Scott. 'Pynchon's Paranoid History'. *Twentieth Century Literature*, 21, 2 (May 1975).

See also the critical articles in *Pynchon Notes* (see above, 'Bibliography', for details).